Welcome to the Th

The idea for this sixty mile route was inspire
journeys of King John between Windsor and
Odiham. A straight line drawn on the map j
Odiham exactly half-way. While many aspe
dramatically in the 800 years since John's ti
can use some of the old ways that he would
variety of attractive scenery - parkland and
along quiet streams and through picturesque villages.

EASY TO FOLLOW
Despite recent development, we can follow a continuous chain of rights-of-way.
With the recent addition of some permitted paths through Crown Estate woodland,
we are able to complete our journey, using less than 5 miles of mainly unclassified
road. The route has good rail connections at the start, middle and end. *(See last
page for a map and travel information.)*

PLAN AHEAD
Plan you walk perhaps over five days. If you are a regular walker, three stages a day
(12 miles) - or even more with light evenings - would be possible. Try to allow time
to explore Windsor and Winchester, as both have so much to offer the visitor. What
gear you take depends very much of the season but walking boots and water-proofs
are always advisable. Keep to a minimum what you carry but remember to plan
ahead. For example, note that between Greywell and Itchen Abbas (a distance of 22
miles) there is only one small shop and one public house actually on the route. You
will need a copy of our WHERE TO STAY leaflet. *(See over page.)*

NO PROBLEMS
At our request Hampshire County Council and the Forestry Commission have made a
number of improvements to the paths but the route is not specially way-marked as
we consider this is unnecessary. Disregard signs indicating other 'named' routes
which sometimes coincide with the Three Castles Path. As we go to press, all the
paths are clear and usable but if you have any problems, or ideas for improvements,
you can help other walkers by contacting the County Council concerned.

AN INVITATION
This is not a strenuous walk - don't let the 'gradient profile' (shown after stage15) put
you off. There are few steep hills to climb, not that many stiles, and rarely much
mud! We suggest this is an ideal 'first long walk' and are confident it will provide
much quiet pleasure and a great sense of achievement to those who take up the
challenge.

CIRCULAR WALKS
Six short circular walks have been included as an introduction to the area through
which our linear route passes.

Reference : ⊖ Bus Stop   P Car Park   P.H. Public House   ❸ Link with circular walk
      C Public Convenience   ☎ Telephone   *i* Information Centre

For further topographical features of the
area see the following Ordnance Survey
maps:

1:50,000 'Landranger' maps:

175   READING & WINDSOR

186   ALDERSHOT & GUILDFORD

185   WINCHESTER

1:25,000 'Pathfinder' maps:

1173	WINDSOR
1189	BRACKNELL
1188	MORTIMER & ARBORFIELD
1204	BASINGSTOKE
1124	LASHAM
1244	ALTON
1243	WINCHESTER (NORTH)
1264	WINCHESTER (SOUTH)

Where and When

WINDSOR
The Castle
Open daily from 10.00
Admission free (except to State
Apartments etc) Tel: (0753) 868286

The Great Park
Open throughout daylight hours
*Large groups of walkers (15 -20 or more)
should contact the Crown Estate Office
beforehand.* Tel: (0753) 860222

ASCOT
The Heath and Race-course
To prevent any Rights-of-Way being
established the Heath is closed to the
public on the first Tuesday in November
each year. Horse racing takes place on
about 23 days throughout the year.
Tel: (0344) 22211.
*On race-days golf is not played so it is
safe to use a very old route known as
Church Path (rather narrow in places)
which runs straight across the Heath towards an avenue of Wellingtonia trees.*

ODIHAM
The Pest House
Cared for and maintained by The
Odiham Society.
Usually open Saturdays and Sundays
throughout the year, 10.30 - 16.00
Admission free - donation welcomed.

The Castle Ruins
Cared for and maintained by Hampshire
County Council.
Usually open at all times.
No admission charge.

WINCHESTER
The Cathedral
Open daily 07.15 - 18.30
Admission free - donation welcomed.
Tel: (0962) 853137

The Great Hall
Open March to Oct Daily 10.00 - 17.00
Nov to Feb Mon - Fri 10.00 - 17.00
Sat - Sun 10.00 - 16.00
Admission free Tel: (0962) 846476

The Hospital of St Cross
Open Summer 09.30 - 12.30, 14.00 - 17.00
Winter 10.30 - 12.30, 14.00 - 15.30
Closed Sundays. Admission £1
Tel: (0962) 842233

TOURIST INFORMATION CENTRES
Windsor
Central Station, Thames Street, Windsor,
Berkshire SL4 1PJ Tel: (0753) 852010
May - Sept Mon - Sat 09.30 - 18.00
Sun 10.00 - 17.30
Oct - April Mon - Sat 09.30 - 17.30
Sun 11.00 - 16.00

The Look Out
Nine Mile Ride, Bracknell,
Berkshire RG12 7QW Tel: (0344) 868222
Open 10.00 - 17.00 daily
*Café (open every day) plus viewing tower
and exhibition (charge).*

Winchester
The Guildhall, Broadway, Winchester,
Hampshire SO23 9LJ Tel: (0962) 840500
May - Sept Mon - Sat 09.30 - 18.00,
Sun 14.00 - 17.00
Oct - April Mon - Sat 09.30 - 17.00,
Sun Closed

Hampshire Borders *Covers N.E. Hants
(Stages 6 - 11)*
Tourist Information Centre,
The Willis Museum, Market Place,
Basingstoke RG21 1QD Tel: (0256) 817618

*The information given above is believed
to be correct at time of publication.*

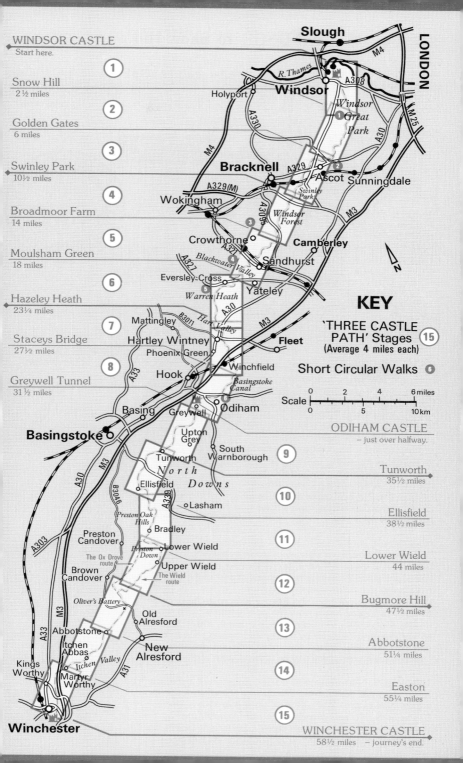

WINDSOR CASTLE
Start here.

① Snow Hill
2½ miles

② Golden Gates
6 miles

③ Swinley Park
10½ miles

④ Broadmoor Farm
14 miles

⑤ Moulsham Green
18 miles

⑥ Hazeley Heath
23¼ miles

⑦ Staceys Bridge
27½ miles

⑧ Greywell Tunnel
31½ miles

Slough

London

M4

R. Thames

Holyport

Windsor

A308

Windsor Great Park

Windsor Great Park ①

M25

A330

A30

M4

Bracknell

A329

Ascot Sunningdale

A329(M)

Swinley Park ②

Wokingham

A309

Windsor Forest

M3

N

③

Crowthorne

A327

Camberley

A327 *Blackwater Valley* ④

Sandhurst

Eversley Cross

Warren Heath ⑤

Yateley

B3011

Hart Valley

M3

Mattingley

Hartley Wintney

Fleet

Phoenix Green

A33

Hook

Winchfield

Basingstoke Canal

KEY

'THREE CASTLE PATH' Stages
(Average 4 miles each) ⑮

Short Circular Walks ⑥

Scale
0   2   4   6 miles
0   5   10 km

ODIHAM CASTLE
– just over halfway.

Basing

Greywell **Odiham**

Basingstoke

M3

A30

Upton Grey

South Warnborough ⑨

Tunworth

North Downs

Tunworth
35½ miles

B3046

Ellisfield ⑩

A339

Ellisfield
38½ miles

Lasham

Preston Oak Hills

Bradley ⑪

Lower Wield
44 miles

The Ox Drove route

Preston Candover

Preston Down

Lower Wield

Upper Wield ⑫

Bugmore Hill
47½ miles

Brown Candover

The Wield route

A303

A33

M3

Oliver's Battery

Old Alresford ⑬

Abbotstone
51¼ miles

Abbotstone

Itchen Abbas

New Alresford

Itchen Valley

A31

⑭

Kings Worthy

Martyr Worthy

Easton
55¼ miles

Winchester

⑮

WINCHESTER CASTLE
58½ miles – journey's end.

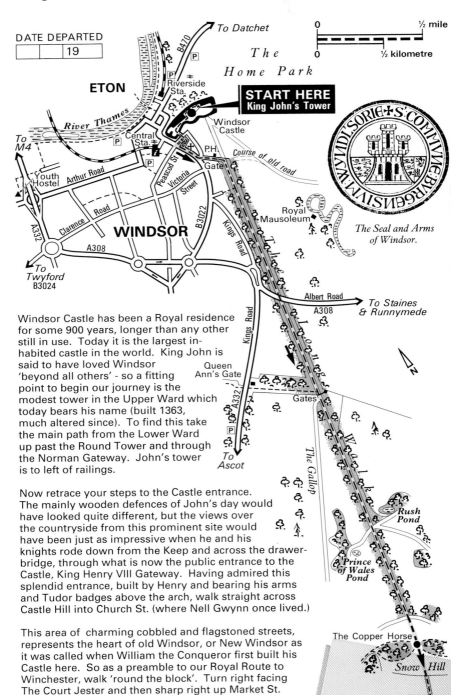

DATE DEPARTED

| | | 19 | |

To Datchet

The Home Park

ETON

River Thames

Riverside Sta.

To M4

Central Sta.

START HERE
King John's Tower

Windsor Castle

Youth Hostel

Arthur Road

Peascod St.

Victoria Street

P.H.

Gate

Course of old road

Royal Mausoleum

WINDSOR

Clarence Road

A308

Kings Road

The Long

Walk

To Twyford B3024

Albert Road
A308

To Staines & Runnymede

The Seal and Arms of Windsor.

Queen Ann's Gate

Kings Road

A332

Gates

P

To Ascot

The Gallop

Rush Pond

Prince of Wales Pond

The Copper Horse

Snow Hill

N

Windsor Castle has been a Royal residence for some 900 years, longer than any other still in use. Today it is the largest inhabited castle in the world. King John is said to have loved Windsor 'beyond all others' - so a fitting point to begin our journey is the modest tower in the Upper Ward which today bears his name (built 1363, much altered since). To find this take the main path from the Lower Ward up past the Round Tower and through the Norman Gateway. John's tower is to left of railings.

Now retrace your steps to the Castle entrance. The mainly wooden defences of John's day would have looked quite different, but the views over the countryside from this prominent site would have been just as impressive when he and his knights rode down from the Keep and across the drawerbridge, through what is now the public entrance to the Castle, King Henry VIII Gateway. Having admired this splendid entrance, built by Henry and bearing his arms and Tudor badges above the arch, walk straight across Castle Hill into Church St. (where Nell Gwynn once lived.)

This area of charming cobbled and flagstoned streets, represents the heart of old Windsor, or New Windsor as it was called when William the Conqueror first built his Castle here. So as a preamble to our Royal Route to Winchester, walk 'round the block'. Turn right facing The Court Jester and then sharp right up Market St.

Windsor Castle and The Long Walk.

Within a few yards, by The Carpenters Arms, turn left into Queen Charlotte St, claimed to be the shortest in Britain, on the left of which stands, or rather leans, the quaintly lop-sided Market Cross House. Then turn left between the Portland stone arches of the imposing Guildhall.

Notice the four columns beneath, but not quite touching, the floor of the Banqueting Hall above. When the architect, Sir Thomas Fitch died soon after building had begun in 1687, supervision of the work was taken over by Sir Christopher Wren. At the request of the townspeople who doubted, it is said, the strength of the design, Sir Christopher inserted these columns. Three hundred years later the four-inch gaps remain.

Shortly pass the Parish Church of St John the Baptist on left then bear left into Park St. and if so inclined, take the last opportunity of refreshment for some miles at the Two Brewers, by Park Street Gate.

Until it was closed in 1851, Park Street continued straight across the Long Walk, to Old Windsor. At that time Queen Victoria purchased land to extend the private Home Park and a new public road was built crossing the Long Walk

much further from the Castle, as we shall soon see.

Go through Park St Gate and turn right to follow the Long Walk. Here you can share, well almost, the Queen's view from the Castle of this impressive man-made vista, stretching invitingly ahead for 2½ miles to the Copper Horse.

The Long Walk was first laid out in 1682, linking the Castle to the Great Park. William III completed planting a double row of elms in 1696, some of which were still standing in 1940. The walk was completely renewed in 1945 with a double row on either side of London planes and horse chestnuts.

Shortly on left, catch a glimpse of a large Mausoleum, which stands in the grounds of Frogmore House, a Royal property since Henry VIII's time. Here lie buried Queen Victoria and Prince Albert.

After nearly a mile, carefully cross the busy A308 and about half-way along the Long Walk, pass through gate in the deer fence, where the surroundings subtly change from manicured parkland to open forest grazing. Now continue ahead to the Copper Horse standing on the highest point in The Great Park - Snow Hill.

Snow Hill to Golden Gates

The commanding bronze statue of George III (known as the Copper Horse), was erected by George IV, in honour of 'the best of fathers'. Sculpted by Richard Westmacott, the 30ft high granite base is modelled on a monument to Peter the Great, in St Petersburg. It is said that before raising the statue in 1831, '16 men got inside, had a luncheon of bread and cheese, drank the King's health and sang God Save the King'.

The Great Park today, although covering 4,800 acres, is only a remnant of Windsor Forest, which at one time included much of Surrey and all of east Berkshire. Much of the Park is open to the public on foot and includes many interesting features, such as Virginia Water, Savill Gardens, Valley Gardens, Smith's Lawn etc. Overall it is an area of great natural beauty and tranquillity, cared for and much loved by successive Monarchs, from 1129, when the first 'Parker' was appointed, to his counterpart today, the Ranger - HRH Prince Philip.

Pass the Copper Horse and continue in same direction. Soon a wide mown strip leads to another gate in the deer fence and a wide grass ride with low hedges either side. After a crossing ride, look left for glimpses of Royal Lodge, a

The Royal Procession at Ascot Gate.

favourite country retreat from 1934 of the Duke of York (George VI) and his family. At end of ride with woodland ahead, continue on rising gravel track (note Ox Pond close by on right), to reach junction of Park roadways. Here turn sharp right, past Chaplains Lodge on left. At fork in road bear left, with fine views sweeping down ahead. At road crossing turn left, to pass 'The Hollies' on left and to follow Duke's Lane, lined by many fine old trees - notice plaque 'Planted about 1751'.

Leave the Great Park by Prince Consort's Gate (1862) and continue along lane, soon to reach public road (B383) at Ascot Gate. Turn right and follow grass verge for 60 yards, then cross road to enter, by a new type of self-closing 'Rambler' gate, tree-lined path with fields of Sunninghill Park close by on both sides. (This is a new path, to replace the right-of-way through the buildings of Home Farm, visible away to right, built in 1990 for the present Duke of York.

The path soon widens into a track. At T junction turn left onto concrete drive, soon becoming tarmac. Where drive starts to bear right, a short diversion to visit Great Pond is possible by turning right onto narrow winding woodland path, crossing wooden footbridge over stream soon to reach the Pond.

The Copper Horse:
- The Copper Horse
- Snow Hill
- Royal Lodge
- Ox Pond
- Chaplains Lodge
- The Hollies
- Windsor Great Park
- Dukes Lane
- Prince Consort's Gate
- To Windsor
- Home Farm
- B383
- Ascot Gate
- To Sunninghill
- Sunninghill Park
- Watersplash Lane
- Shop
- **Cheapside**
- Great Pond
- Norfolk Gates
- Golden Gates
- Cheapside Road

0   ½ mile

The Copper Horse

Retracing your steps, continue to end of drive at East Lodge and then turn right along footway (Cheapside Rd).

The white painted gates shortly on right are used by the procession of landaus, conveying HM The Queen and her party, as it drives along the course each day of the Royal Ascot race-meeting in June. Soon you may see through the trees the twin lodges and ornamental Norfolk Gates (1955) which mark the beginning of the New Straight Mile course.

Where the road forks by Silwood Park Nurseries, bear left, shortly to reach the impressive Golden Gates. At end of railings to left of gates, turn right to enter enclosed path alongside race-course.

The Golden Gates and adjoining Lodge (a listed building), were erected in 1879 at the start of the original straight mile course, which is no longer used for racing, partly because it is out of sight from the stands. The tall concrete posts along the side of the path here, had wires strung between them across the course to prevent enemy planes from landing during the last war.

Follow side of course and at junction, turn right along road (A330 Winkfield Rd). Cross lines of both old and new Straight Miles, then immediately turn left between white posts.

Waiting to cross the course.

If racing is in progress you may be held up for a few minutes on the road or crossing the course, but there is public access to Ascot Heath even on race-days. This world-famous race-course was laid out in 1711 to the orders of Queen Anne who, like her present-day namesake the Princess Royal, was an enthusiastic horse-woman, keeping a pack of Buckhounds at nearby Swinley Bottom.

Within a few yards of leaving the road, pass Golf Club-house, go through gate in fence and gap in running rails, to cross the lush turf of the course itself. Turn right along service road then presently branch left onto narrower tarmac drive - crossing golf course with care. Pass cricket pavilion on right then cross fair-way and race-course to reach road (A322).

Cross into Kennel Avenue (lined with fine Wellingtonias) and in front of Huntsmans House, turn left into Burleigh Rd. (Queen Anne's Buckhounds were kennelled near here). Follow footway on right, and at end of new houses turn left, still along Burleigh Rd. At top of slope, shortly before road junction, turn right into byway (Blythewood Lane), which descends to road (A329).

Here turn right, and just after Gainsborough Drive cross main road using central reservation. Follow verge and turn left at wooden gate into Englemere Pond Nature Reserve. At lake edge turn right along woodland path, keeping pond close by on left. Path soon widens to a track (Butterfly Ride). At

crossing path, (left for nature trail - right for car park), continue ahead to reach road (Swinley Rd) opposite Whitmore Cottages.

Cross road, turning left over railway bridge and at bottom of slope turn right through stile-way to enter Swinley Park - part of the Crown Estate. Shortly, at junction of forest rides, turn sharp left along broad grass ride, to follow Permitted Path sign, (the first of several over the next 1¹/₂ miles). Where drive merges from left (Windsor Ride) continue ahead, now on tarmac, and at top of rise stay on drive turning right.

About 300 yards beyond this bend, notice immediately to right, a semi-circle of 12 old lime trees which probably marked the turning circle for carriages bringing Royal hunting parties in the 18th century from Windsor Castle to Swinley Lodge, which stood nearby until about 1825. Some of the trees here, and elsewhere in the Park, show traces of a

Swinley Park.

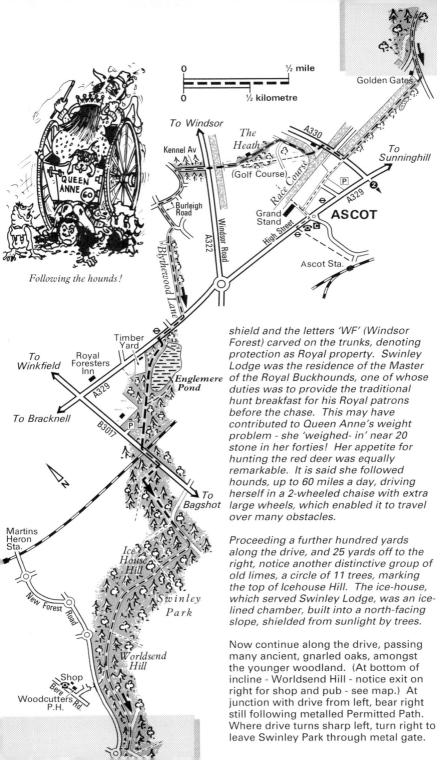

0 ½ mile

0 ½ kilometre

Following the hounds!

QUEEN ANNE 60

To Windsor

Kennel Av

The Heath (Golf Course)

Golden Gates

A330

To Sunninghill

Burleigh Road

Windsor Road

Blythewood Lane

A322

Race Course

Grand Stand

High Street

P

A329

ASCOT

2

Ascot Sta.

Timber Yard

To Winkfield

Royal Foresters Inn

A329

Englemere Pond

To Bracknell

B3017

P

To Bagshot

N

Martins Heron Sta.

Ice House Hill

New Forest Road

Swinley Park

Worldsend Hill

Shop

Bere

Woodcutters Rd.

P.H.

shield and the letters 'WF' (Windsor Forest) carved on the trunks, denoting protection as Royal property. Swinley Lodge was the residence of the Master of the Royal Buckhounds, one of whose duties was to provide the traditional hunt breakfast for his Royal patrons before the chase. This may have contributed to Queen Anne's weight problem - she 'weighed- in' near 20 stone in her forties! Her appetite for hunting the red deer was equally remarkable. It is said she followed hounds, up to 60 miles a day, driving herself in a 2-wheeled chaise with extra large wheels, which enabled it to travel over many obstacles.

Proceeding a further hundred yards along the drive, and 25 yards off to the right, notice another distinctive group of old limes, a circle of 11 trees, marking the top of Icehouse Hill. The ice-house, which served Swinley Lodge, was an ice-lined chamber, built into a north-facing slope, shielded from sunlight by trees.

Now continue along the drive, passing many ancient, gnarled oaks, amongst the younger woodland. (At bottom of incline - Worldsend Hill - notice exit on right for shop and pub - see map.) At junction with drive from left, bear right still following metalled Permitted Path. Where drive turns sharp left, turn right to leave Swinley Park through metal gate.

Stage 4 **Swinley Park to Broadmoor Farm** 3½ miles

After leaving Swinley Park, cross ditch to roadside (New Forest Rd) and turn left along grass verge. Just beyond roundabout cross road using central reservation and continue in same direction along pavement to cross footbridge spanning dual carriageway (A322). Pass Coral Reef swimming pool on right and 25 yards past car-park entrance, turn left to cross road with care (Nine Mile Ride B3430). Follow entrance drive through car park to main buildings of The Look Out.

This building was opened by HM The Queen in April 1991, together with public access to a series of walks, trails and rides through some 2,600 acres of Windsor Forest. This is very much a 'working forest', producing about 15,000 tons of timber each year, mainly Scots Pine, for use as sawn logs, fencing materials, telegraph poles and pulp for paper-making. Don't miss the unusual viewing tower - before the trees grow any higher!

Walk to left of The Look Out, passing picnic area, cross broad track and go half right across clearing. At path crossing go straight ahead, (signposted 'Heritage Trail') along broad sandy track. Ignore

two left-hand forks and after rise, at crossing track, with bank on right, turn right. After 100 yards bear left onto wide grassy ride. Continue ahead at next crossing (Ladies Mile) and on reaching T junction, turn left, now with young trees on right, soon to reach and turn right along a wide track - The Devil's Highway.

This is the route of the Roman road from London to Silchester (via Staines), so called, it is said, by the tribes that lived here after the Romans went home, because they thought only the devil could have built a road so straight!

In this area are remains of several military redoubts - raised banks with outer ditches. These were built around 1792 for training purposes, against the threat of possible invasion by Napoleon's forces, and were the scene of large-scale military exercises at that time.

Suspension footbridge over dual carriageway.

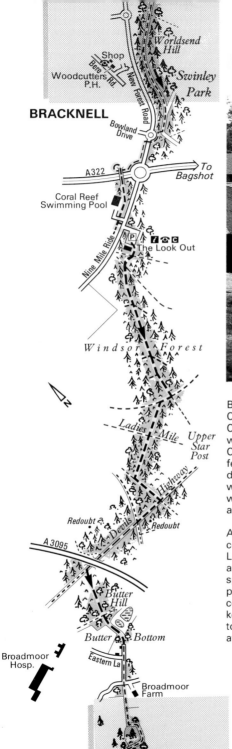

Worldsend
Hill

Shop

Woodcutters
P.H.

Bere Rd

New Forest Road

Swinley
Park

BRACKNELL

Bowland
Drive

A322

→ To
Bagshot

Coral Reef
Swimming Pool

Nine Mile Ride

P

The Look Out

W i n d s o r   F o r e s t

N

Ladies   Mile

*Upper
Star
Post*

Highway

Redoubt

Devils

Redoubt

A 3095

*Butter
Hill*

Butter   Bottom

Broadmoor
Hosp.

Eastern La

Broadmoor
Farm

Beyond metal gate (marking end of Crown Estate and beginning of Forestry Commission land) continue ahead along wide, dipping sandy track to pass under Crowthorne bypass. Shortly, at end of fence on left, turn left along path descending through light woodland, with Butter Hill on left. Pass between wooden posts and shortly reach ponds at Butter Bottom.

After metal gate with cottage on right, continue along road, becoming Eastern Lane, with views of Broadmoor Hospital away to right. (Built in 1863, it is a special hospital, providing treatment for psychiatric patients under secure conditions.) Where road turns right, keep straight on over stile by metal gate to pass buildings of Broadmoor Farm away on left.

0	½ mile

0	½ kilometre

Leaving Broadmoor Farm follow path ahead through two fields with wire fence on right, turning left and right through woodland, finally to cross stile and turn right along tree-lined track. At end of track, cross stile and road, to go ahead up bank into light woodland, with green metal fence on left. At end of woodland strip cross ditch and turn left.

This area is Owlsmoor Bog and, shortly, Edgbarrow Woods, an SSSI covering 78 acres - one of the few remaining heathlands in Berkshire. There are some rare plants, birds and insects to be found here.

At cross path turn right along prominent gravel path, parallel with overhead cables away to left. At end of woodland (Edgbarrow Woods) cross road with care (Crowthorne Road), to take the path bearing left between metal posts, down through trees and under cables. Stay on slowly descending sandy path until end of woodland where properties appear on left and then houses on right. This is Sandy Lane and you have reached Little Sandhurst, which boasts at the time of writing, two pubs, two general stores and a Post Office.

Notice Fox & Hounds on left (corner of Hanscombe Rd) and 120 yards further

down lane, immediately after No. 13 'Woodfall', turn right down tarmac path. At bottom turn left (Grampian Rd) and then right (Chiltern Rd). Round left-hand bend, at No. 33 turn right along path between houses, to bear left into woodland ahead. Follow path, with wire fence on left, then just before open field, turn left through metal swing gates and carefully cross railway line to enter National Trust woodland - Ambarrow Hill. (For details see Ramble 4)

Within 50 yards of the railway turn left through stile-way to enter grounds of one-time Victorian mansion - Ambarrow Court - now a Country Park. On reaching tarmac path, turn right and follow left and right bends to reach car-park. Carefully cross road (A321) and pass stile-way into path through light woodland. At road, within a few yards turn left onto short path and pass through kissing gate. Follow ditch along side of field, passing buildings of Ambarrow Farm away on right. At end of second field cross lane with kissing gates either side, to enter meadow with lake ahead.

Keep lake nearby on right. Then pass close to solitary oak tree and shortly join wooden walk-way. Bear right in front of

Near Broadmoor Farm.

swing gate and within 35 yards pass through gate and turn right to follow path alongside Blackwater River, the county boundary between Berkshire and Hampshire.

You are now in the Blackwater Valley, which extends for some 12 miles between Eversley and Aldershot, along the Hampshire border with Berkshire and Surrey. The path has been created as a result of 'planning gain' linked with the extraction of gravel. Three of the four lakes on the right will form a nature reserve of some 90 acres, to be managed by BBONT, the local naturalists' trust. Special planting and landscaping will encourage wildfowl and wader species. Two public viewing hides will be provided.

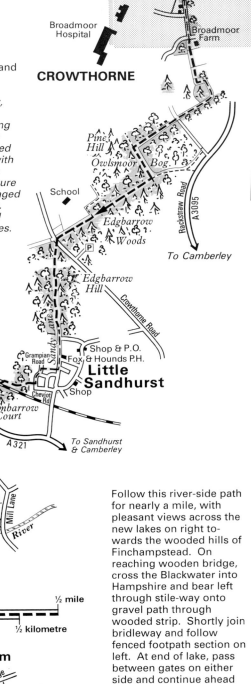

Follow this river-side path for nearly a mile, with pleasant views across the new lakes on right towards the wooded hills of Finchampstead. On reaching wooden bridge, cross the Blackwater into Hampshire and bear left through stile-way onto gravel path through wooded strip. Shortly join bridleway and follow fenced footpath section on left. At end of lake, pass between gates on either side and continue ahead along gravel track to reach road at Moulsham Green.

Stage 6 **Moulsham Green to Hazeley Heath** 5¼ miles

At Moulsham Green turn right along road, cross Blair Park Rd and turn right along edge of Green. Facing properties, turn right then left on drive and enter narrow tarmac path to left of house No. 23 ahead. Cross two minor roads and at metal rails keep right, shortly to cross wooden footbridge and stile. Follow left side of small triangular field and at far corner bear left into farm track, shortly turning right, to enter field on left by stile near metal gate. Follow right-hand side of field, passing buildings of Watmore Farm. Cross stile in corner and turn left along Fox Lane, leading to main road (A327).

Immediately cross road, turning left, and within a few yards turn right over ditch to follow right-hand edge of field (a headland path) through two fields to reach road with large house ahead (Firgrove Manor). Turn right along road, carefully cross Marsh Lane (B3016) soon to reach hamlet of Up Green.

The group of three Victorian Gothic cottages facing you at road junction (and three more in the district) were built around 1899, regardless of expense it would seem, by one John Martineau as a memorial to the famous writer, Charles Kingsley, who was vicar of nearby Eversley. They must be the grandest labourers dwellings ever built!

Relief portrait of Charles Kingsley.

Now turn right along Chequers Lane and within a few paces, immediately after 'Reed Field', turn left along tarmac drive between houses. At end of gardens cross stile, follow path keeping woodland (Lower Eversley Copse) on left. Pass to left of green metal gate into narrow path with fence on right. At end of vineyard on right, cross sleeper bridge and stile, then continue ahead for 35 yards. Here turn left along edge of large field, with trees on left. At top of field cross stile to left of gate and immediately turn right to follow fence on right. Cross two more stiles to reach road. Go straight across green ahead and join lane, passing on right The Old Manor and St Mary's Church. (See Ramble 5).

Continue past The Old Rectory to end of lane. Immediately after unusual metal gate-posts, turn left to follow rising path, which marks the beginning of the Forestry Commission's Warren Heath, part of Bramshill Forest. A few yards before emerging from canopy of trees, bear left to follow wide gravel path, with plantation of young trees (Corsican Pines - planted 1974) on right and mature woodland to left. Shortly the track bears slightly right into the young plantation to reach junction of several forest tracks.

Besides allowing additional free public access on foot, the Forestry Commission has agreements which provide for more esoteric pursuits here such as horse riding, carriage driving, motor rallying and dog-sledding - although not all at the same time!

Go straight ahead (crossing Welsh Drive), past concrete 'viewpoint' on right, to follow very wide 'haul road'. At next crossing (Sir Richard's Ride) continue ahead, bearing right, with expansive open area at present on left.

This open area has been excavated for gravel and hoggin, and is now reclaimed for tree planting, using the recently developed 'ridge and furrow' technique. After back-filling with top-soil and silt the land is ridged instead of being levelled as in the past. The result is a dramatic improvement in survival and growth of the young trees.

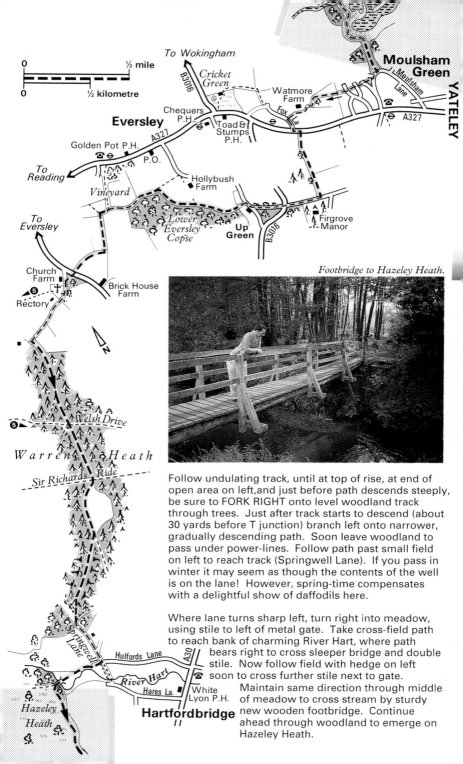

Map labels

To Wokingham

B3306

Cricket Green

Watmore Farm

Moulsham Lane

Moulsham Green

YATELEY

Chequers P.H.

Eversley

Fox Lane

A327

A327

Toad & Stumps P.H.

Golden Pot P.H.

A327

P.O.

To Reading

Vineyard

Hollybush Farm

Lower Eversley Copse

Up Green

B3306

Firgrove Manor

To Eversley

Church Farm

Brick House Farm

Rectory

N

Welsh Drive

Warren Heath

Sir Richards Ride

Springwell Lane

Hulfords Lane

A30

River Hart

Hares La.

White Lyon P.H.

Hartfordbridge

Hazeley Heath

Footbridge to Hazeley Heath.

Follow undulating track, until at top of rise, at end of open area on left, and just before path descends steeply, be sure to FORK RIGHT onto level woodland track through trees. Just after track starts to descend (about 30 yards before T junction) branch left onto narrower, gradually descending path. Soon leave woodland to pass under power-lines. Follow path past small field on left to reach track (Springwell Lane). If you pass in winter it may seem as though the contents of the well is on the lane! However, spring-time compensates with a delightful show of daffodils here.

Where lane turns sharp left, turn right into meadow, using stile to left of metal gate. Take cross-field path to reach bank of charming River Hart, where path bears right to cross sleeper bridge and double stile. Now follow field with hedge on left soon to cross further stile next to gate. Maintain same direction through middle of meadow to cross stream by sturdy new wooden footbridge. Continue ahead through woodland to emerge on Hazeley Heath.

Stage 7 **Hazeley Heath to Stacey's Bridge** 4¹/₄ miles

Reaching Hazeley Heath, turn left and follow path through light woodland, undulating and at times uneven, with open heathland stretching away to right. Where path rises steeply take the centre, steepest path. Emerging from trees, turn left along broad gravel path, now with woodland on left.

At end of broad track, where paths meet at clearing, continue ahead, forking slightly left towards mature woodland. Winding path descends gradually through mixed woodland, through swing gate and then along gravel path past houses, finally to reach road (Hunts Common). Turn right and at end of green cross main road (A30), with great care and maybe some difficulty!

Enter Park Corner Rd, with golf course on left, shortly to reach green and duck-pond with picture-book Causeway Farm beyond.

Having admired the ducks, turn right through middle of green, following line of old oaks. Cross minor road to follow wide grass verge between cricket ground and, naturally, The Cricketers. Cricket has been played on the Green here for over two hundred years. Cross another minor road and maintain same direction along the middle path of three ahead. Carefully cross A323 into Green Lane

and immediately after St John's Church, turn left. At end of railings take centre of three paths ahead through open trees (The Mildmay Oaks), to reach road by drive to Vicarage.

The rows of mature oak trees, which are such a feature of the open greens running through the middle of Hartley Wintney, were planted after the Napoleonic Wars, for patriotic purposes, by the then Lady of the Manor, Lady Mildmay. The speedy development of iron and steel naval vessels meant that the oaks were spared.

Continue along footway soon bearing right into Church Lane. Just before Cottage Green (Rd) cross road onto grass verge fronting house 'Meadow Way'. After kissing gate follow path in field, parallel to road, crossing drive to Wellfield House. After next field enter burial ground adjoining St Mary's Church.

Turn left, then right along gravel path around three sides of burial ground and old churchyard, to enjoy the splendid view over what were once the common fields of the medæval village. Just after small brick outbuilding exit left through squeeze-way at corner and pass through woodland strip, alongside lane.

The Basingstoke Canal.

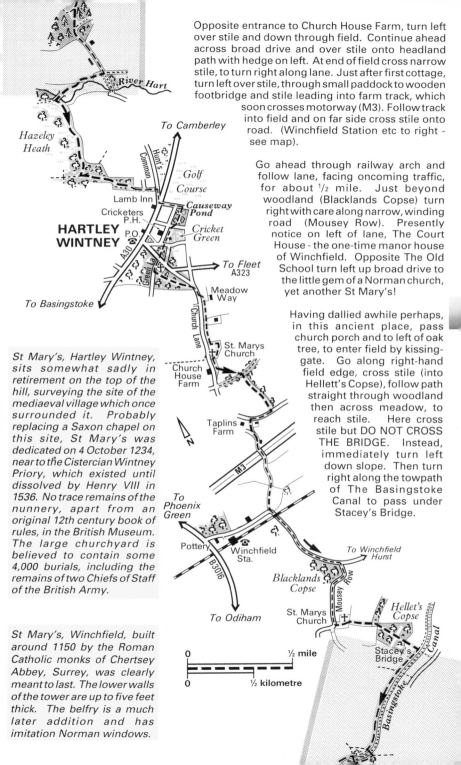

Opposite entrance to Church House Farm, turn left over stile and down through field. Continue ahead across broad drive and over stile onto headland path with hedge on left. At end of field cross narrow stile, to turn right along lane. Just after first cottage, turn left over stile, through small paddock to wooden footbridge and stile leading into farm track, which soon crosses motorway (M3). Follow track into field and on far side cross stile onto road. (Winchfield Station etc to right - see map).

Go ahead through railway arch and follow lane, facing oncoming traffic, for about ½ mile. Just beyond woodland (Blacklands Copse) turn right with care along narrow, winding road (Mousey Row). Presently notice on left of lane, The Court House - the one-time manor house of Winchfield. Opposite The Old School turn left up broad drive to the little gem of a Norman church, yet another St Mary's!

Having dallied awhile perhaps, in this ancient place, pass church porch and to left of oak tree, to enter field by kissing-gate. Go along right-hand field edge, cross stile (into Hellett's Copse), follow path straight through woodland then across meadow, to reach stile. Here cross stile but DO NOT CROSS THE BRIDGE. Instead, immediately turn left down slope. Then turn right along the towpath of The Basingstoke Canal to pass under Stacey's Bridge.

St Mary's, Hartley Wintney, sits somewhat sadly in retirement on the top of the hill, surveying the site of the mediaeval village which once surrounded it. Probably replacing a Saxon chapel on this site, St Mary's was dedicated on 4 October 1234, near to the Cistercian Wintney Priory, which existed until dissolved by Henry VIII in 1536. No trace remains of the nunnery, apart from an original 12th century book of rules, in the British Museum. The large churchyard is believed to contain some 4,000 burials, including the remains of two Chiefs of Staff of the British Army.

St Mary's, Winchfield, built around 1150 by the Roman Catholic monks of Chertsey Abbey, Surrey, was clearly meant to last. The lower walls of the tower are up to five feet thick. The belfry is a much later addition and has imitation Norman windows.

Stage 8 **Stacey's Bridge to Greywell Tunnel** 4¹/₂ miles

The 200 year old Basingstoke Canal originally ran 37 miles from Basingstoke to the Wey Navigation at Byfleet, to carry farm produce, timber and chalk to the London Docks, returning with coal and fertiliser. It was never a commercial success, only being kept afloat as it were, in Victorian times by carrying construction materials for the railways and the military camp at Aldershot. The last barge moored at Basingstoke Wharf in 1910. Today, ownership is shared between Surrey and Hants County Councils. Restoration for leisure began in 1973 - officially re-opened May 1991.

Our route now follows the canal towpath for about 4¹/₂ miles to reach the tunnel at Greywell, with possible detours en route. Try the high-level path on the opposite bank between the third bridge (Sprat's Hatch) and the fourth. Returning to towpath look to right (at end of woodland on opposite bank) for small lake - Wilks Water and a few yards around it, 'King John's Hunting Lodge' (N.T. but not open to the public). Further along at Colt Hill is the Water Witch - a canal-side pub - also access to Odiham. By next road bridge over canal are The Swan pub and a garage with shop.

Since Saxon times Odiham had been a Royal manor, no doubt a convenient stopping place between Windsor and Winchester, being a day's journey from each. With discontent amongst the English barons and the threat of a French invasion, King John chose Odiham as a site for one of four new castles. Between 1207 and 1214, at the 'enormous' cost of £1100, John built a strong-hold and a home.

Then, just beyond swing bridge, across the field immediately on right, catch your first glimpse of the ruined keep of King John's Castle, half-way point on our journey.

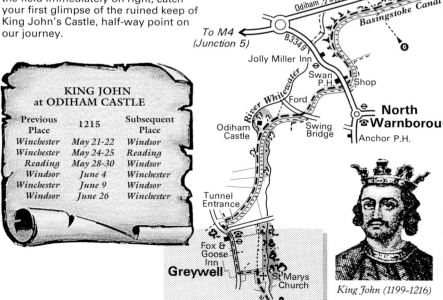

KING JOHN
at ODIHAM CASTLE

Previous Place	1215	Subsequent Place
Winchester	May 21-22	Windsor
Winchester	May 24-25	Reading
Reading	May 28-30	Windsor
Windsor	June 4	Winchester
Winchester	June 9	Windsor
Windsor	June 26	Winchester

King John (1199-1216)

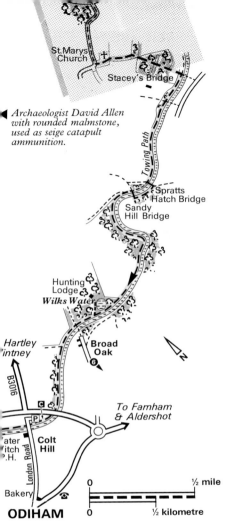

St.Marys Church

Stacey's Bridge

Archaeologist David Allen with rounded malmstone, used as seige catapult ammunition.

Towing Path

Spratts Hatch Bridge

Sandy Hill Bridge

Hunting Lodge
Wilks Water

Hartley Wintney

Broad Oak 6

B3016

To Farnham & Aldershot

ater itch .H.

London Road

Colt Hill

Bakery

ODIHAM

0   ½ mile

0   ½ kilometre

N

After King John died, Odiham Castle and the surrounding Royal Park continued to provide excellent deer hunting for his successors. Eleanor, his youngest daughter, inherited the Manor and lived here for 30 years with her second husband, the influential baron, Simon de Montfort.

Detailed household accounts have survived and provide some fascinating information about life in those days. For instance, on March 17th 1265, 1,000 plates were bought for 6s8d! In 1321 some £248 was spent , which included the purchase of no less than 95,350 roof tiles, 3,000 'stones' and 17 tons of lead.

Although no traces remain today, many buildings were constructed in and around the Castle during those years, to accommodate the often large numbers of men and horses who had to be housed from time to time. On one occasion, 334 horses were stabled there or grazing in the nearby meadows.

Castles prolonged wars, but didn't finish them. As the decades went by, the Kings and no doubt their Queens, wanted greater comfort than the ageing castle could provide. Also, the importance of Winchester was declining in the 1400's, which lessened the usefulness of Odiham.

Although we associate the Castle mainly with King John, it was used at some time by every English King of the 13th and 14th centuries. As we gaze today, nearly 800 years after it was first built, at the ruined tower, it is still a potent reminder of the once vibrant and successful mediæval fortress which played a prominent part for more than 250 years through a turbulent period of English history.

We can only wonder whether it was a fine summer's day when, on June 15th 1215, King John rode out of his Castle and turned his horse towards Runnymede, and the Magna Carta which awaited him.

Just beyond the Castle ruins, the Whitewater River flows under the canal and a 'winding hole', enables barges to turn around before reaching Greywell Tunnel, now ahead of you.

The central feature, the remains of which we see today, was an unusual octagonal, three storeyed tower. Its' walls of flint were ten feet thick, with wide buttresses. The twenty acre site was carefully chosen within a loop of the Whitewater River. The marsh and water meadows between the moat and the river could be easily flooded in times of danger. This was put to the test, successfully, in 1216 when a handful of the King's men - 3 knights, 3 squires and 7 men-at-arms were confronted by an army led by Louis, son of the French King. This small garrison held out for 15 days before surrendering, on condition that they retained their freedom, their horses and their arms.

The Greywell Tunnel (1230 yards) was a long way for the bargemen who had to 'leg it' from end to end. The steps down to the canal-side at this point enable us, with care, to peer into the gloom beyond the tunnel entrance, with its' iron grill. In 1932 the roof collapsed some 140 ft below Greywell Hill. As a result the draught-free, dark interior, maintains a constant temperature of 10°C, providing a perfect environment for the estimated 2,000 bats which hibernate here, attracted from within a radius of 30 miles.

Follow path over tunnel entrance to reach stile at roadside. Turn right then left at T junction to pass 'Fox & Goose'.

On right, notice the large timber-framed, wisteria-clad building - The Malt House - was originally called Kiln House, due to the two hop kilns which form one end. The house is Elizabethan and the wisteria is reputed to be 150 years old.

Immediately before Church Cottage ahead, turn left through lych-gate to reach St Mary's Church in its idyllic riverside setting.

Church Cottage is possibly older than The Malt House, also timber-framed with brick infilling. It is thought to have been the Priest's lodging, and is said to be haunted.

St Mary the Virgin, like many village churches which we admire today, has ancient origins and yet owes much of its appearance to later centuries. In this instance, from its Norman doorways (notice the one bricked up on the south side), to the chancel, rebuilt in 1870, with flint facing and stone quoins (corner stones). The walls of the nave and tower are both 12th century. Inside, an interesting feature is the 16th century carved oak rood screen.

At church porch turn right past tower and large oak to leave churchyard over stile. Follow raised wooden walk-way (built by Hampshire Recreation at our suggestion) to reach grassy bank of Whitewater and, shortly, delightful old Greywell Mill. At this point our route turns right, away from the river, but do first follow path to left of water-wheel to

view the mill pond in its tranquil setting.

It is rather sad to think, that after a mill of some sort has stood here for over a thousand years, since Saxon times, it was only about sixty years ago that milling literally 'ground to a halt'. The remains of the old breastshot wheel can be seen, where the weight of water from Mill Head continues to pour down, as though striving to turn once more the now paddle-less wheel. In 1933 the mill was brought to a standstill by a mechanical fault, which was never repaired.

The last miller here, one Donald Jabez Dean, then turned his hand to growing watercress for Covent Garden and continued to live in this idyllic spot for over fifty years. (Max Bygraves once made a film here, but you won't want to know about that!)

The Whitewater continues to flow on, to join the Loddon, and then finally the Thames, leaving the old mill to slumber peacefully in its retirement. How many miller's daughters may have dallied on this riverbank in a thousand years?

Retrace your steps and follow track away from mill. After gate, and 30 yards before junction with road ahead, turn left over stile then right to follow field edge, using stiles to keep hedge and road (Upton Grey Rd) on right. This recently diverted path climbs slowly to reveal extensive views across this western end of the North Downs. Continue to follow hedge then fence through large fields, eventually to reach stile into crossing track - summer route of the historic Harrow Way - at Four Lanes End. Turn right and cross Upton Grey Rd, to follow the Harrow Way with fields on right and trees on left. The Way shortly crosses a small valley, to reach Five Lanes End, marked by a group of fine old beech trees.

From this isolated meeting of ancient tracks, turn left. Just after Dutch barn on the right, a Roman road once crossed our path - difficult to imagine, perhaps, in this remote spot. Where surfaced track swings right, keep straight on, along grassy track, eventually to reach road.

The River Whitewater at Greywell.

Turn right along open road. Pass Tunworth Hill Cottages, descend hill and go ahead at cross roads. Notice old Post Office cottage and the one-time school-master's cottage with school-room attached. Soon bend in lane reveals sweeping entrance to Old Rectory. To visit the tucked-away little church of All Saints, look out for gate at end of white picket fence on left. A line of old beech trees leads to the church past the walls of Manor Farm. Returning to lane, turn left to pass Manor Farm.

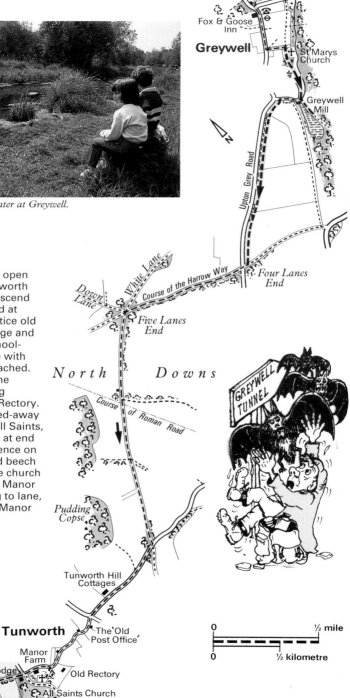

After Manor Farm on left, when lane bends right, go straight ahead on track, with hedges and fields both sides. Follow this clear track for about a mile, with fields on left and, later, areas of woodland on right (Hackwood Park), to reach Winslade Farm. Follow farm drive to main road - A339.

Here turn left along verge and shortly with care cross road to fork right along track, passing pair of cottages.

The substantial embankment ahead carried the Basingstoke & Alton Light Railway from 1901 to 1936. It was never a viable enterprise; the 12 mile journey took nearly an hour, so it was quicker to go by pony and trap!

Beyond arch notice isolated one-time Methodist chapel tucked away to right. Where track reaches gateway, go straight ahead to follow bridleway along bottom of valley, keeping woodland (Whinkneys Copse) on left.

path straightens into a hollow tree-lined track (Alley Lane), and reaches, rather surprisingly, the highest point of our journey to Winchester - 646 feet. Eventually the path widens before reaching road at - Ellisfield.

(To visit the one village pub, The Fox - about ½ mile away - turn right here and take the footpath from just beyond the church, across the fields to the south - see map.)

The villagers describe Ellisfield as 'heaven on earth' - and who would argue? Hopefully, you will have time to sample some of its delights. Turn right along Church Lane and view the duck pond through the 'hole in the wall', by the Old Manor. The pond wall was built in 1939 by General Nesbit, which was NOT a popular idea at the time!

On the right along here is the Memorial Hall and then Church Cottage (the one-time Post Office). The hall has been the centre of social activity since it was opened in 1920. Can you imagine U.S. servicemen, in full battle-dress, dancing here with the local girls before de-camping from the village to take part in the D-Day Normandy landings? The troops were 'under canvas' on Preston Oak Hills, which our route crosses.

Photo: The British Library.

◀ *King, hunting in the forest. From a 13c. painting.*

Some 200 yards before far end of field, cross stile in wooden rails and maintain same direction through corner of woodland. Join grass ride sloping up towards open field and then follow headland with woodland (Allwood Copse) on right. Where track turns right into woodland, keep straight on along narrow path still following line of field but now in light woodland. This winding

The village takes its name - once Aelle's Field - from King Aelle, who landed in Sussex in 477 AD. But the Church of St Martin is rather more modern, celebrating its 700th anniversary only recently. Long before the church was built, what is now Church Lane was the preferred winter (high ground) route of that ancient track the Harrow Way, which we first encountered at Four Lanes End.

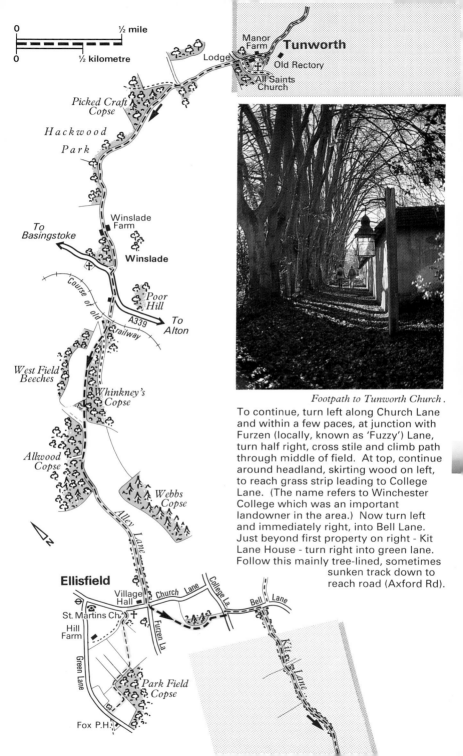

Tunworth
Manor Farm
Lodge
Old Rectory
All Saints Church

Picked Craft Copse

Hackwood Park

Winslade Farm

To Basingstoke

Winslade

Poor Hill

Course of old railway

A339

To Alton

West Field Beeches

Whinkney's Copse

Allwood Copse

Webbs Copse

Alley Lane

Ellisfield

Village Hall — Church Lane — College La. — Bell Lane

St. Martins Ch.

Hill Farm

Furzen La.

Green Lane

Park Field Copse

Fox P.H.

Kit Lane

0 ½ mile
0 ½ kilometre

N

Footpath to Tunworth Church.

To continue, turn left along Church Lane and within a few paces, at junction with Furzen (locally, known as 'Fuzzy') Lane, turn half right, cross stile and climb path through middle of field. At top, continue around headland, skirting wood on left, to reach grass strip leading to College Lane. (The name refers to Winchester College which was an important landowner in the area.) Now turn left and immediately right, into Bell Lane. Just beyond first property on right - Kit Lane House - turn right into green lane. Follow this mainly tree-lined, sometimes sunken track down to reach road (Axford Rd).

Leaving the end of Kit Lane carefully cross the road ahead (Axford Road) and take new bridleway opposite. Follow this rising path straight up through the mixed woodland (Preston Oak Hills), keeping field nearby on left. At path junction at top of hill, turn left along bridleway soon to reach road. Here turn right and within a few yards left into Spain Lane, with row of fine beech trees on left. At end of beeches, turn right along broad grassy track, with hedge on left at first. This easy-going path takes us downhill for about 1¹/₂ miles, threading its way between woods and fields until eventually, the appearance on left of a pretty thatched cottage, heralds our arrival at the hamlet of - Bradley.

At this point there is a choice of routes; either along The Ox Drove (see panel on facing page), or the more varied way, described below, through the attractive villages of Bradley, Lower and Upper Wield.

Turn left along lane into Bradley, following right-hand bend to pass neat village duck pond. At this point, look back to see the small flint-faced church of All Saints, looking down from the nearby slopes.

This tiny village experienced some notoriety when King Charles I claimed the Manor to settle a debt of £1001.1s. The occupier, one Thomas Taylor, refused to give possession and for several months held out against various attempts to take it by modest force. Finally, in early 1630, the aptly named Sheriff, Sir Henry Wallop, sent to London for the 'great guns' and with a force of 200 men, destroyed the house. Exit Thomas Taylor.

Follow road round left-hand bend, alongside garden of Pond Cottage almost concealed beneath its thatch. Then turn right on gravel track, becoming wide grass path, through avenue of sycamore trees. Soon continue on broad headland, with large open field on left and valley just visible through trees close-by on right. Continue over top of incline and descend towards valley ahead. Half-way down edge of field, turn left through middle of field towards corner of woodland (Park Copse), and follow chalky headland path alongside wood on left into corner of field.

Go left through swing gate, to cross end of copse and reach stile after 100 yards. Maintain same direction across large field towards point about half-way along cable on horizon. Cross stile next to metal gate and bear slightly right across corner of this smaller field. Then bear right again along headland, keeping wire fence and line of trees on left. At end of field go through small wooded strip to stile.

Cross farm track and stile ahead into garden of Nicholas Farmhouse. Cross lawn between flower beds to further stile. Bear half left through middle of small paddock and over stile into another garden. Pass immediately to right of white house (Whites Farm) across patio. (This is the public Right-of-Way!) A rustic arch leads to gravel drive and within a few yards turn right along 'high street' of Lower Wield.

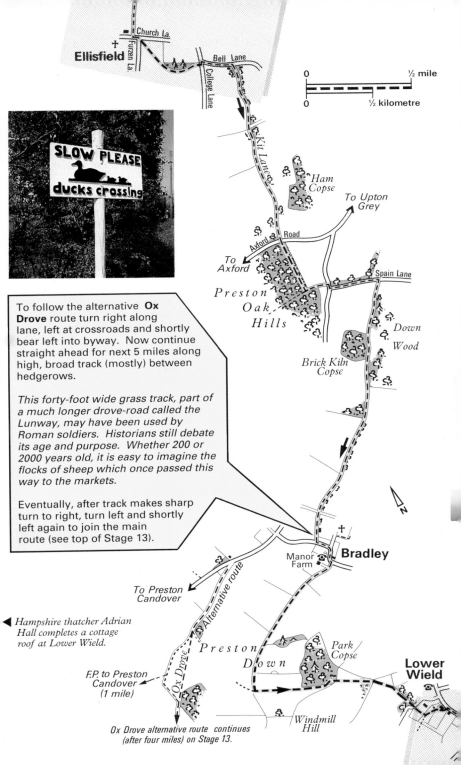

Church La.

Furzen La.

✝ **Ellisfield**

Bell Lane

College Lane

0 ½ mile

0 ½ kilometre

Kit Lane

Ham Copse

To Upton Grey

Axford Road

To Axford

Spain Lane

P r e s t o n

O a k

H i l l s

Down Wood

Brick Kiln Copse

To follow the alternative **Ox Drove** route turn right along lane, left at crossroads and shortly bear left into byway. Now continue straight ahead for next 5 miles along high, broad track (mostly) between hedgerows.

This forty-foot wide grass track, part of a much longer drove-road called the Lunway, may have been used by Roman soldiers. Historians still debate its age and purpose. Whether 200 or 2000 years old, it is easy to imagine the flocks of sheep which once passed this way to the markets.

Eventually, after track makes sharp turn to right, turn left and shortly left again to join the main route (see top of Stage 13).

✝

Manor Farm

Bradley

To Preston Candover

Alternative route

◀ *Hampshire thatcher Adrian Hall completes a cottage roof at Lower Wield.*

P r e s t o n

D o w n

Park Copse

Lower Wield

F.P. to Preston Candover (1 mile)

Ox Drove

Windmill Hill

Ox Drove alternative route continues (after four miles) on Stage 13.

On reaching metalled road at Lower Wield turn right to pass several cottages including 'The Windmill', (a one-time inn of this name). Where lane turns right, continue ahead through garden to reach entrance into field. Descend mid-field path, bearing right, to stile on far side and, within a few yards, to lane.

On the right here is the delightful Yew Tree Inn. The original cottage - the part next to the even older yew tree - was built beside a chalk pit some 300 years ago. By the 1850's it was a beer-house, and now today an attractive pub/restaurant, saved from extinction, like many a country inn, by the motor car.

To continue, cross lane and go straight up headland path, catching glimpses of cricket field and later valley, through trees on right. At end of field on left cross stile and bear slightly left to follow the natural line of path directly towards cluster of trees. Follow enclosed path between hedges to soon reach Upper Wield village green, passing one-time school, now the village hall, on left. Stay on right of green, towards thatched cottages.

On our right as we cross the green stands Wield House (early 19th century). Only the porch now remains of the previous house on this site, built in 1580/85 by William Wallop, one-time MP, twice Mayor of Southampton, whose family connection with the area stretches from Saxon times to the present day. Imagine the scene, one day in 1591, when Queen Elizabeth I and her household forming a great procession, arrived here, to take refreshment no doubt, on route from the Marquis of Winchester's house of Abbotstone, to stay with Sir Henry Wallop, William's brother, at Farleigh Wallop.

At this point our route continues straight ahead through the village but the old church certainly merits a visit, so on the far side of the green cross road and take first turning right. Just after Church Cottage on left, with village stores ahead, turn left into churchyard.

St James Church contains a fine memorial to William Wallop (and his third wife), Wield's most famous son. The church was built about 1150 at the direction of the Conqueror's grandson, Henry de Blois, Bishop of Winchester and is a fine example of a small Norman church of that period. It was probably thatched in earlier days, and until 1810 had a tower, which was found to be unsafe. This was replaced by the present wooden belfry to house the one surviving bell, two others having to be sold to help pay for the cost of repairs. The interior is full of interesting features, like the 12/13th century Purbeck marble font, installed here in 1900, having been discovered in the garden of a house in

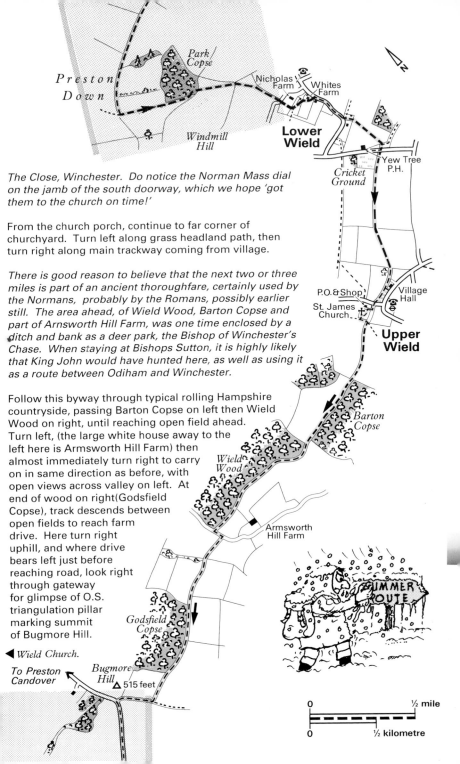

The Close, Winchester. Do notice the Norman Mass dial on the jamb of the south doorway, which we hope 'got them to the church on time!'

From the church porch, continue to far corner of churchyard. Turn left along grass headland path, then turn right along main trackway coming from village.

There is good reason to believe that the next two or three miles is part of an ancient thoroughfare, certainly used by the Normans, probably by the Romans, possibly earlier still. The area ahead, of Wield Wood, Barton Copse and part of Arnsworth Hill Farm, was one time enclosed by a ditch and bank as a deer park, the Bishop of Winchester's Chase. When staying at Bishops Sutton, it is highly likely that King John would have hunted here, as well as using it as a route between Odiham and Winchester.

Follow this byway through typical rolling Hampshire countryside, passing Barton Copse on left then Wield Wood on right, until reaching open field ahead. Turn left, (the large white house away to the left here is Armsworth Hill Farm) then almost immediately turn right to carry on in same direction as before, with open views across valley on left. At end of wood on right(Godsfield Copse), track descends between open fields to reach farm drive. Here turn right uphill, and where drive bears left just before reaching road, look right through gateway for glimpse of O.S. triangulation pillar marking summit of Bugmore Hill.

◀ Wield Church.

To Preston Candover

Map labels:

Preston Down
Park Copse
Windmill Hill
Nicholas Farm
Whites Farm
Lower Wield
Cricket Ground
Yew Tree P.H.
P.O.& Shop
Village Hall
St. James Church
Upper Wield
Barton Copse
Wield Wood
Armsworth Hill Farm
Godsfield Copse
Bugmore Hill △ 515 feet

SUMMER ROUTE

0   ½ mile
0   ½ kilometre

Where farm drive meets road, turn left down hill. At bottom of slope go 30 yards BEYOND end of field on right before turning right onto track which climbs through middle of broad woodland strip. After admiring the view from the top of hill continue along winding track bearing left through plantation (Spy Bush) to finally reach T junction. On turning left along this hard, stony track (Spybush Lane), we rejoin our alternative route via The Ox Drove.

For the next three miles we also share the Wayfarers Walk - which runs for 70 miles, from Emsworth on the coast to Inkpen, on the Berkshire Downs.

At bottom of slope pass drive to Swarraton Farm. Go straight on, over wooded hill-top, descending by grassy track to reach Oliver's Battery, a relatively modern name for an iron age hill fort site, on Abbotstone Down. Cross road (B 3046) to pass picnic area where a Hampshire Recreation board tells all. Leaving parking area, continue along gravel track and where this swings right, keep straight on across open grassy strip, soon with wire fence on left. Path narrows through edge of Sheep Wood and then continues with hedge and ditch on left and open fields on right. Signpost just before isolated farmyard shows evidence, for the first time, of our destination - 'Footpath to Winchester'.

Continue ahead on track, still with hedge on left and open field on right. With buildings ahead (Abbotstone Farm), at junction with track descending from right, bear left downhill.

Away on the hilltop to our left (see map) is the site of a once thriving mediæval village, which commands fine views of the surrounding countryside. A stony track on left, leads to a road on the hilltop, from where a circle of trees on a raised bank marks the site. The Black Death (1348/9) may have been the start of the village's decline; eighty years later there were less than ten households left.

This almost empty landscape conceals a lively past. The valley was the meeting point of several ancient trackways, important routes from Saxon times to the later Middle Ages.

To our right, Abbotstone Farm was the hillside site chosen by William Paulet, 1st Marquis of Winchester, for the timber-framed mansion he built in the 16th century. Was it the situation or the hospitality which brought Queen Elizabeth I here, from Winchester, on three separate occasions?

By the late 1600's the Tudor house was in disrepair. In 1685, Charles Paulet, 6th Marquis of Winchester (soon to become 1st Duke of Bolton) started to build a

To Preston Candover

Godsfield Copse

Bugmore Hill △ 515 feet

Farm

Ox Drove

Alternative route

F.P. to Brown Candover ½mile

F.P. to Totford ¾mile

To Alresford

Spybush Lane

Spy Bush Plantation

STAGE 13!! I KNEW WE SHOULD HAVE CALLED IT 12 A!

Swarraton Farm

Oliver's Battery

To Alresford

P C

B3046

Abbotstone Down

To Totford & the Candovers

Sheep Wood

great new brick mansion, just above the old house. The writer, Daniel Defoe described 'a very handsome, beautiful palace'. The Duke died in 1699 and the house was never finished. By 1800 almost all traces of the Duke's great house had disappeared. By 1900 the Great Garden was the farm rick-yard. Today, the only feature Queen Elizabeth might recognise would be the oak beams in the farmhouse bedrooms!

Both the track we are on and the road past mediæval village, lead down to the hamlet of Abbotstone.

Route of Wayfarer's Walk

N

0 ½ mile

0 ½ kilometre

Abbotstone Farm

R. Candover

Abbotstone

Site of Medieval Village

◀ *Straight on, over Itchen Stoke Down.*

At Abbotstone follow the road over a stream - the Candover - with cottages on right. Where road divides, go straight ahead into hedged track, the antiquity of which is suggested by its' width. Five similar tracks meet at top of hill ahead where we go straight on, over Itchen Stoke Down. This was once open downland. It became very famous between 1770 - 95, as the venue for some historic cricket matches played here for high stakes, as much as 500 and 1000 guineas. Now continue on narrower path for a mile to reach road, shortly after crossing one-time railway.

This line, closed in 1973, once linked Alton to the main line at Winchester. The section between Alton and Alresford has been preserved as a steam railway - the Watercress Line.

Turn right along road for 20 yards, then right again over stile to climb meadow, following line of mature trees round left-hand bend. Leave field by gate and join short estate road. Turn right at lane ahead and after 50 yards turn left up bank to follow narrow hedged path. Path turns left and right before joining drive at 'Little Hayes' on left. Pass Primary School and at bottom of slope turn left through village of Itchen Abbas. At main road (B3047) follow footway turning left. Dependent on your inclination, and the time of day, either continue ahead for a few yards to the

Plough Inn, or cross road at bus stop and fork right towards Avington, to reach lych-gate of St John's Church.

Author Charles Kingsley (see Ramble 5) came here to fish in what he called 'the loveliest of vale rivers', and also wrote part of The Water Babies while staying in the village. Kingsley may well have seen the re-building of St John's in 1863. All that remains of the earlier Norman church are the Chancel Arch and the ornamental stone over the doorway of the porch. The timber framing of the barrel vaulted roof is an impressive example of Victorian craftsmanship.

In the shade of the venerable church-yard yew tree lies John Hughes, a gypsy sentenced to death at Winchester Assizes in 1825 for horse stealing, the last man to be hanged for this offence in England. Due to the forgiving nature of the then Rector, Robert Wright, who owned the horse, the body was buried in consecrated ground.

Facing the lych-gate, take the track to right and shortly pass through swing-gate into delightful enclosed path with meadows sloping down to the Itchen. Cross avenue of old limes through swing gates and continue straight ahead, eventually to reach lane at Chilland.

There is an intriguing tradition that the Danes built boats on the banks of the

Itchen and that their word 'keillandt', meaning 'where keels are laid', became corrupted into Chilland. Our Saxon ancestors paid Danegeld to these invaders for a bit of peace and quiet. We still pay it today - and get delicious bacon in exchange!

For a 'cameo' of this idyllic Itchen scenery walk down the lane a few yards to the old water-mill. Within living memory local farmers brought produce here to be ground for animal fodder - notice the iron ring on the wall for tethering horses. Later, the buildings were used for a time as a trout hatchery, to stock this famous fishing stream. The ford here was used by horse traffic until early this century.

To continue, take narrow fenced path on other side of lane, in same direction as before. At end of small paddock on left cross stile, bearing left, to pass through three fields, heading straight towards the spire of St Swithun's Church, Martyr Worthy.

This is a very old path, probably the one referred to by Samuel Speed, a one-time Rector, as existing in 1654.

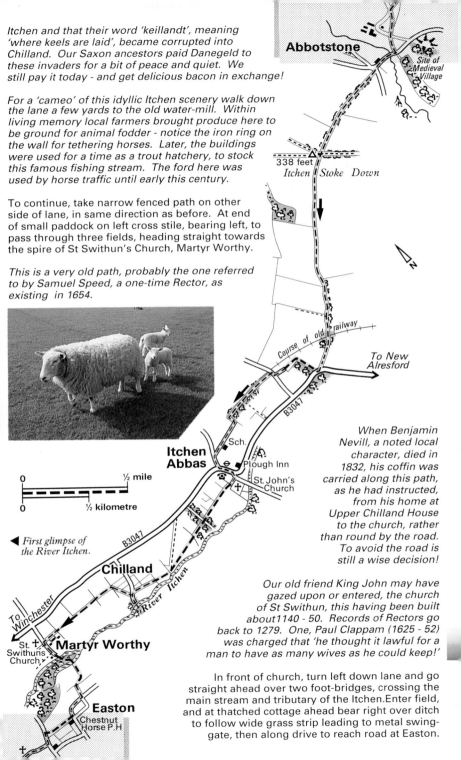

First glimpse of the River Itchen. ◀

When Benjamin Nevill, a noted local character, died in 1832, his coffin was carried along this path, as he had instructed, from his home at Upper Chilland House to the church, rather than round by the road. To avoid the road is still a wise decision!

Our old friend King John may have gazed upon or entered, the church of St Swithun, this having been built about 1140 - 50. Records of Rectors go back to 1279. One, Paul Clappam (1625 - 52) was charged that 'he thought it lawful for a man to have as many wives as he could keep!'

In front of church, turn left down lane and go straight ahead over two foot-bridges, crossing the main stream and tributary of the Itchen. Enter field, and at thatched cottage ahead bear right over ditch to follow wide grass strip leading to metal swing-gate, then along drive to reach road at Easton.

Map labels:

Abbotstone
Site of Medieval Village
338 feet
Itchen Stoke Down
N
Course of old railway
To New Alresford
B3047
Sch.
Itchen Abbas
Plough Inn
St. John's Church
B3047
Chilland
River Itchen
To Winchester
St. Swithuns Church
Martyr Worthy
Easton
Chestnut Horse P.H

0 — ½ mile
0 — ½ kilometre

At Easton, turn right and follow road round left-hand bend. With 'Chestnut Horse' just ahead, turn right into narrow fenced path along side of pub. Cross stile into field and with fence on left, bear to right of farm buildings, to leave field over stile in front of cottages. Turn left along road and shortly bear right into Church Lane.

Beyond the Church of St Mary, and the Old School House, turn right through metal gate into one-time school field. Go diagonally through this field then across meadow to reach river. Follow right-hand side of two fields to enter wooden-railed path leading under motorway. On other side of M3, follow right-hand wooden fence where it turns sharp right. Once again we are closely following the Itchen.

On reaching a drive, the right-of-way to the right affords an excellent opportunity if you have the time, to enjoy again the river scenery; a series of footbridges carry the path from the nearby, pretty Fulling Mill cottage, over a labyrinth of streams to reach the villages of Kings Worthy, Abbots Worthy and even Headbourne Worthy - all very Worth-while!

Continuing along the riverside path, follow fringe of trees on right. Where Easton Down sweeps up to left, carrying its' noisy 20th century burden, follow the twisting path down and under two road bridges (limited headroom - duck or grouse!) It is now a matter of keeping 'eyes right' for a while, to concentrate attention on natural beauty and not man's contribution. Follow fence on right for about one mile, until leaving narrow end of final field over stile, and along farm track to reach Easton Lane.

Here turn right, soon becoming Wales Street and about 100 yards after aptly named public house, 'First In - Last Out', turn right between Nos. 11 & 13 to continue in same direction, along riverside path. Stay close to the stream, along the gardens of Water Lane, to the Youth Hostel (part of the Town Mill, National Trust) and junction with Bridge Street. You are now in the heart of Winchester, for centuries the capital of Saxon England.

Carefully cross road, turn right and immediately beyond 18th century St Swithun's Bridge, turn left down steps to The Weirs. Within a few yards notice plaque recording only visible section of the City's Roman wall.

Where path divides, fork right and soon right again, following the impressive flint wall of Wolvesley Castle, (built in 1138 by Henry de Blois, Bishop of Winchester, but reduced to a shell in the Civil War).

Continue ahead along College St, passing Winchester College, the famous public school, founded in 1382 by William of Wykeham. The school motto is well known: 'Manners makyth Man'. But not so polite, is the Latin inscription on one of the old buildings which translates as 'Learn, Leave or be Licked'!

At end of College St turn right through Kingsgate, or more fully, 'St Swithun upon Kingsgate'. The tiny mediæval church, first mentioned in 1263/4, is built over the arches. Immediately turn right again, through another gateway, into The Close, with the exceptionally beautiful houses of Cheney Court on right. At end of building on left, bear left towards the Cathedral, and pass under flying buttresses (a necessary 20th century addition) to reach the West Door.

This masterpiece of mediæval masonry was pieced together in various architectural styles during the 450 years from 1079. King Henry III was baptised here, Richard the Lion Heart was crowned here, Queen Mary I was married here, Jane Austen and Isaak Walton are buried here. Truly a treasure house of English history.

With your back to the Cathedral walk diagonally across the Square shortly passing through covered way to reach and turn left up High Street. At top, in front of Westgate turn left up Castle Hill to finally reach the hilltop site of Winchester Castle and across the cobbled yard the splendid mediæval Great Hall.

Since 1967 excavations have been going on here to reveal the secrets of the castle which William the Conqueror ordered to

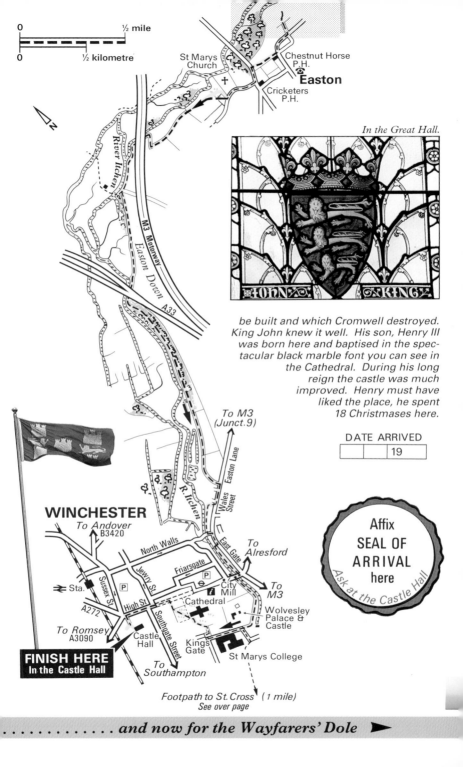

0 ½ mile
0 ½ kilometre

St Marys Church

Chestnut Horse P.H.

Easton

Cricketers P.H.

River Itchen

M3 Motorway

Easton Down

A33

In the Great Hall.

HONX · KING

be built and which Cromwell destroyed.
King John knew it well. His son, Henry III
was born here and baptised in the spec-
tacular black marble font you can see in
the Cathedral. During his long
reign the castle was much
improved. Henry must have
liked the place, he spent
18 Christmases here.

To M3
(Junct.9)

Easton Lane

DATE ARRIVED

| | 19 |

Wales Street

R. Itchen

WINCHESTER

To Andover
B3420

North Walls

East Gate

To
Alresford

Affix
**SEAL OF
ARRIVAL**
here

Ask at the Castle Hall

Friarsgate

Jewry St.

Sussex St.

Sta.

High St.

A272

P

P

City Mill

Cathedral

To
M3

Wolvesley
Palace &
Castle

To Romsey
A3090

Southgate Street

Castle
Hall

Kings
Gate

St Marys College

FINISH HERE
In the Castle Hall

To
Southampton

Footpath to St. Cross (1 mile)
See over page

. . . . *and now for the Wayfarers' Dole* ➤

The Wayfarer's Dole

Given the time and energy, a fitting conclusion to this Three Castles walk, is to follow our old friend 'Ichen Streeme' for just one more mile, through the water meadows south of the City to St Cross. Here you may still knock at the Porter's Lodge to claim the Wayfarer's Dole - a 'horn' of ale and some bread - once provided for 100 poor men every day.

The Hospital of St Cross and Almshouse of Noble Poverty, to give it its full title, has been described as the finest and grandest surviving almshouse of the Middle Ages in England, still serving the original purpose. St Cross was founded in 1136 by Henry de Blois, Bishop of Winchester (the Conqueror's grandson) to provide a safe haven for 13 elderly gentlemen. In the 15th century a new
foundation was set up - the Almshouse of Noble Poverty - to provide for 'those who had once had everything handsome about them, but had losses'. Since then 27 Brothers have occupied the terrace of tall-chimneyed houses built in 1446 along one side of the quadrangle.

St Cross is reached by retracing our steps past Winchester College, then turning right to follow the signposted route along College Walk and the riverside path. Finally, bear right through field in front of the unmistakable mediæval buildings, to enter Britain's oldest charitable institution.

If you've journeyed with us on foot these many miles from Windsor, we think you can fairly claim a little hospitality. Savour the Wayfarer's Dole!

Path Gradient PROFILE

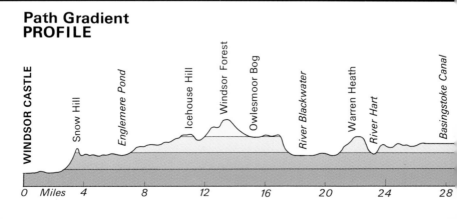

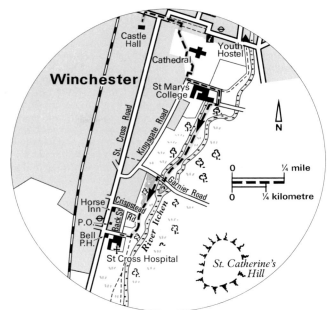

*Authors
David Bounds and
Dave Ramm at St Cross.*

◀ *St Cross, from the quadrangle.*

Contact Addresses for Footpath Matters

BERKSHIRE
Recreation and Access Group
Highways & Planning Dept., Shire Hall,
Shinfield Park, Reading RG2 9XG

HAMPSHIRE
County Recreation Department,
North Hill Close, Andover Road,
Winchester SO22 6AQ

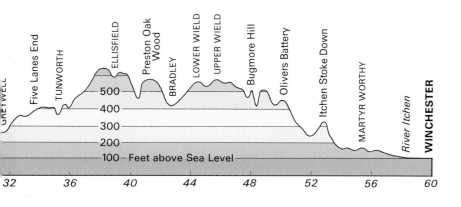

Cranbourne Tower and theVillage

This circular walk in the western part of Windsor Great Park, includes impressive distant views of Windsor Castle, and the opportunity to visit the Copper Horse, with its' fine views down the Long Walk. Please observe the Regulations displayed at entrances to the Park.

Distance: about 4 miles
OS Map: Pathfinder 1173 'Windsor'
Start: Parking area on Sheet Street Road (A332) opposite Cranbourne Gate (Grid ref. 947727)

With your back to main road and Cranbourne Gate, follow narrow tarmac road with fenced field on left and woodland of Great park on right, to reach at top of rise, the red brick Cranbourne Tower.

The Tower is the oldest building in the Park, thought to have been built about 1500. Samuel Pepys and John Evelyn both record having stayed here in 1665 and 1673 respectively, in those days a much larger property. Most of it was demolished in 1861, retaining one large room at least, used by Queen Victoria during her carriage drives around the Park. On 3 May 1764 a horse was foaled here during a solar eclipse. Appropriately named 'Eclipse', it was to become one of the most famous race-horses of all time, being unbeaten in its' 18 races.

From the 'Crown Estate - Private' sign, retrace your steps about 65 yards and fork left across grass to follow minor paths through woodland, keeping paling fence close on left. A bridle route runs parallel on right. On reaching broad crossing track with field beyond, look for distant view of Windsor Castle. Turn right along track and in about 80 yards merge with sandy bridleway, to continue in same direction, keeping fence nearby on left.

Follow this bridleway, through left hand bend along edge of woodland. On emerging from trees, turn right on grass path, along edge of woodland at first, then tarmac drive, to reach main road.

Between here and our starting point at Cranbourne Gate, some 13 acres were planted with oaks in 1580. Many of these can still be seen.

With care cross main road and about 25 yards after passing through Rangers Gate, fork left on climbing grass path passing woodland and then fenced field on left. At bottom of descent, enter double fenced track with Russell's Pond on right. On shortly reaching tree-lined avenue - Queen Anne's Ride - turn right along avenue to reach road ahead.

Queen Anne's Ride was planted in 1703, one of several rides cut through the Park to facilitate the Queen's enthusiasm for following her Buckhounds. This particular ride, led directly at that time to the Royal Kennels which the Queen had built at Swinley Bottom, adjoining Ascot Heath.

Turn left along road, and after passing through gate of Deer Park, bear right up slope to follow winding track, then where fence on right turns right, keep straight on through trees to soon reach the Copper Horse - the statue of King George III and the Long Walk.

The Long Walk. In 1682 a warrant was issued for the purchase of land 'to make an avenue 240 ft wide between our Castle of Windsor and the Great Park there'. (See stages 1 & 2).

Turning your back to the Castle, pass just over brow of hill to see Royal Lodge, the pink washed building amongst distant trees to left. Royal Lodge has been used by the Queen Mother as a country retreat since she and the Duke of York first moved there in 1934. Now descend to pass through gate in deer fence into broad hedged grass ride. After just over 200 yards, turn right into another ride (closed to horses) to reach road ahead. Turn left along road for about 150 yards to end of fenced field (Richardsons Lawn) on right. Here turn right across grass to reach road and houses at edge of The Village.

This model village was started in 1948 when 32 houses and a general stores & post office were built. (An opportunity perhaps to purchase refreshments here!) Further houses were added in 1954 and 1966.

Turn right along road, cross Queen Anne's Ride and pass recreation ground on left. After pond on left, turn right at cross-roads and on reaching further cross-roads at 'The Prince Consort Drive 1860' sign, turn left along road to return to start.

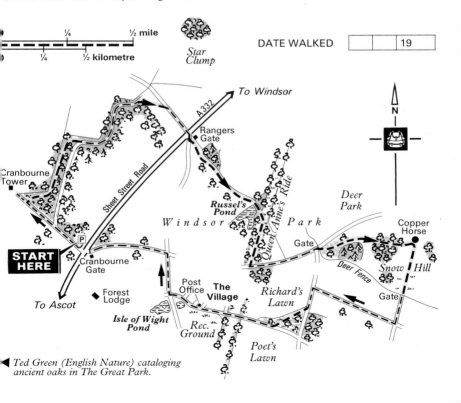

DATE WALKED [ ] [19]

◀ Ted Green (English Nature) cataloging ancient oaks in The Great Park.

Tom Green's Field and Silwood Park   Ramble 2

This walk follows footpaths and tracks in the historic parish of Sunninghill, where it is still possible to take a quiet country walk between the fingers, as it were, of an increasingly built-up area.

Distance: 4 miles
OS Map: Pathfinder 1189
          'Bracknell and Ascot'
Start: Car Park at eastern end of
          High St (A329), which is free
          for public use except on race-
          days. (Grid ref. 926688)

Leave car-park, carefully cross High St, turning left to follow footway. Turn first right into St George's Lane and follow road round left-hand bend, to pass St George's School.

Notice the earlier Victorian building, once called St James's School, which the young Winston Churchill knew well as a prep-school boarder here in 1882/4 - apparently he hated it! Today it is a girl's school.

Continue down gravel track and at bottom of slope turn sharp right (Wells Lane). Soon pass sports ground - the

area on left along here used to be known as Sunninghill Bog but now, cleared and drained, is put to more productive uses, hence the current name - St George's Fields.

Bear left at T junction of tracks and pass under railway arch to reach St George's Lane. Turn left, and immediately fork left along tarmac path with wooden fence to gardens on right. Pass through second barrier and turn left along Lower Village Rd, under railway bridge. At end of fence on left, by entrance to 'Combe Meadows', turn left into Combe Lane. About 50 yards beyond last big house on right, 'Coombe Grange', turn right through gap in fence to enter Tom Green's Field - a picnic area. (This name commemorates a late chairman of the Parish Council, during whose term of office in the 1970's, the field was purchased to preserve it from development.)

Follow the middle path through light woodland, past tennis courts on right and then along track to left of Victory Field - a memorial to the men who lost their lives in WW1. (The field was

Shady path near St Micheals Church.

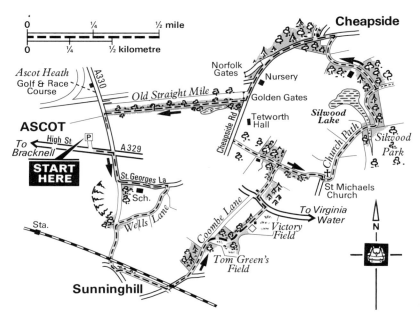

landscaped 'by hand' during the depression of the 1920's, when the men were paid 6d per hour.)

At main road cross carefully, turning left along footway. At end of wall turn right into narrow path alongside garden of Wellsbridge Cottage, to reach T junction of paths. Before turning right at this point, it is an interesting diversion to turn left for some 150 yards to cross Hog Brook, notable for its' perpetual brown colour, caused by an algae. Beyond the stream, away to the right across parkland, stands the recently renovated Tetworth Hall, currently owned by a successful hotelier. Now retrace your steps straight along this path to soon reach St Michael's Church.

The Parish Church we see today was restored in 1824 but there has been one on this site since 1199. The remarkable hollow yew tree here, with its' iron girdle, is claimed to be over 1000 years old.

Walk through the churchyard, with its ornate monuments and into the lane leading around the church, past the burial ground, through a kissing gate and along a wide strip between fields - known as Church Path. At bottom of

slope pass kissing gate and follow slowly rising path with views of Silwood Lake away to left. A few yards beyond high metal gate on right (private path to Silwood Park), turn left into narrow enclosed path.

Silwood Park is today a Field Station for Imperial College of Science and Technology. The timber-framed old building to left of path along here is the one-time farmhouse and barn of Silwood Park estate.

Exit onto roadside by well-preserved kissing and carriage gates, the latter complete with unusual latch. Cross (Cheapside Rd), turning left along footway. Cross end of Watersplash Lane and then drive-way to Sunninghill Park at East Lodge. (For interesting details about this particular spot see end of Stage 2.) Where the road forks, by Silwood Park Nurseries, bear left to shortly reach the impressive Golden Gates. At end of railings to left of gates, turn right to enter enclosed path alongside race-course. At junction with road (A330 Winkfield Rd) turn left to return to start.

DATE WALKED | | 19 |

Heathlake and Gorrick Woods

This easy, gentle walk takes full advantage of the woods and forest remaining on the northern fringe of the much developed village of Crowthorne, and includes the seven acre lake set in fifty acres of woods of Heathlake Park, now in the care and protection of Wokingham District Council.

Distance: about 4 miles (2 mile
           alternative)
OS Map: Pathfinder 1189
           'Bracknell and Ascot'
Start: Small Car Park at Heathlake
           Park, off Nine Mile Ride
           (Grid ref. 828653)

Facing Heathlake, follow path from car park along right-hand side of lake. Pass behind boathouse and continue through tall trees, still with lake nearby on left. At footbridge - WHICH DO NOT CROSS - turn right along tarmac path for a few yards. Continue ahead on broad grass strip for 75 yards before turning right along estate path between gardens. Shortly cross road, passing to right of No. 24 and continue in same direction. At T junction turn right along broad tree-lined path (Oaklands Lane). With care cross fairway of golf course into tree-line path. Shortly, look out for path to turn right at end of wood on right, now with small playing-field on left.

Join tarmac path to Ravenswood Village Settlement - a charitable foundation caring for adults and children with learning disabilities. PLEASE KEEP DOGS ON LEAD through this area. On reaching main drive, turn left along it. Soon notice building with small clock pinnacle, above rose garden. This contains an attractive café and mini-market, open to passers-by. Where drive divides, keep straight on along track and turn right onto path behind stables. Eventually, where path forks, keep left to shortly reach road-side. FOR SHORTER WALK take right fork and follow woodland path straight ahead to reach car park at start.

To continue longer walk carefully cross road, opposite Kingsbridge Cottages,

turning right along footway to soon reach the quaintly named 'Who'd a Tho't It'. Turn left along gravel path to left of pub to enter playing field, with its' splendid modern sports pavilion (St Sebastians Playing Field Trust). Turn left across near corner of playing field, to pass through stileway and turn sharp right along edge of woodland (part of Bramshill Forest). At path junction, where playing field on right ends, turn left along broad track. At next path junction, continue ahead, now with woodland both sides. At end of this block of trees, bear right along broad track through cleared area, to soon re-enter established woodland along a straight track, at first gently descending.

At wooden posts across track, continue ahead into narrower path with dense evergreens (Yews) on right. A house comes into view away to left (Gorrick Cottage) and then shortly, at T junction, turn right to pass metal gate. Stay on this wide forest track to finally leave, at wooden posts - Gorrick Woods.

Cross road ahead, and continue in same direction along roadway (Hatch Ride), soon to pass on right Heathlands Riding Centre. Beyond here, the road narrows to a path, to soon reach busy road near roundabout. Here turn sharp right along tarmac footway. Where this joins roadside, cross carefully, to re-enter Heathlake Park by stile in boundary fence. Within a few paces, turn right for 25 yards and then left (in front of white post) for 30 yards. Here, at T junction, turn right and within a few yards bear left onto wide path, soon descending gently, still through trees. At bottom of slope, on reaching path junction, turn right to follow path through trees with lake close-by on left, to soon return to car park.

DATE WALKED | | 19 |

Winter at Heath Lake.

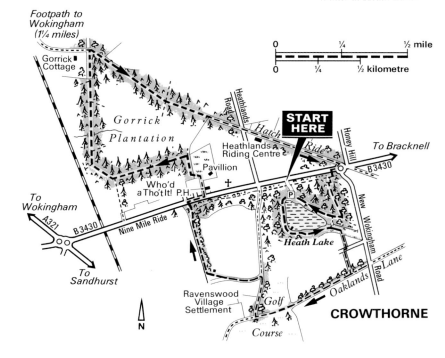

Footpath to
Wokingham
(1¼ miles)

Gorrick
Cottage

0   ¼   ½ mile

0   ¼   ½ kilometre

Gorrick
Plantation

Heathlands
Road

Hatch Ride

START
HERE

Honey Hill

To Bracknell

B 3430

Heathlands
Riding Centre

Pavillion

Who'd
a Tho'tIt! P.H.

P

To
Wokingham

A 321

B 3430

Nine Mile Ride

Heath Lake

New Wokingham Road

To
Sandhurst

Ravenswood
Village
Settlement

Golf

Oaklands Lane

CROWTHORNE

Course

N

Blackwater Valley and Spout Pond

This walk crosses varied countryside between the Blackwater River and the delightful National Trust and adjoining woodland, of Finchampstead Ridges.

Distance: about 4 miles
OS Map: Pathfinder 1189 'Bracknell and Ascot'
Start: Car Park at Ambarrow Court Countryside Park (Grid ref. 825626) which can also be reached easily by footpath from Crowthorne Station. (See map Stage 5)

With back to car park carefully cross road (A 321) and pass through stile-way onto footpath along edge of woodland strip. On reaching road, within a few yards turn left onto short path to enter field through wooden swing-gate. Follow ditch along edge of two fields, passing buildings of Ambarrow Farm away to right. At end of second field, cross lane with kissing gates either side, to enter meadow with lake ahead. This land and the lake on right are intended for uses such as sailing, canoeing and board-sailing. However, development of the site has not begun.

Keep lake nearby on right. Then pass close to solitary oak tree and shortly join wooden walk-way. Bear right in front of swing gate and within 35 yards pass through gate and turn right to follow path alongside Blackwater River, the county boundary between Berkshire and Hampshire.

You are now in the Blackwater Valley, which extends for some 12 miles between Eversley and Aldershot, along the Hampshire border with Berkshire and Surrey. Since 1979 the Local Authorities and others have been developing facilities for a wide range of activities in the valley, including walks, boating, fishing etc. Three of the four lakes on the right will form a nature reserve of some 90 acres, to be managed by BBONT, the local naturalists' trust. Special planting and landscaping will encourage wildfowl and wader species. Two public viewing hides will be provided.

Follow the riverside path for nearly a mile, with pleasant vistas across the

lakes towards the wooded hills of Finchampstead. On reaching wooden bridge over Blackwater, continue ahead on same bank but now with bridleway on riverside. Path soon turns right, to leave river. Cross small wooden bridge (on bridleway) and then bear right through stile-way to follow left-hand edge of meadow with lake (to which there is access at this point), on right. At end of field, pass by gate and cross car park. Turn left along lane (Lower Sandhurst Rd) and take first turning on right into Dell Rd. Just beyond second property, South Ridge, turn right at wooden barrier to enter the National Trust woodland of Finchampstead Ridges. Follow footpath between bridleway on right and ditch. Where path rises, go straight on, leaving fork to left, soon descending to pass on left - Spout Pond.

Finchampstead Ridges is one of the National Trust's earliest acquisitions. The first 60 acres of woodland were purchased by public subscription in 1913 for £3,000, part of the Bearwood estate owned by Mr John Walter, a Berkshire MP and proprietor of The Times newspaper. In 1863 Mr Walter had constructed the road over The Ridges and planted the Wellingtonia Avenue, still a splendid sight today. In more recent years, gifts of adjoining woodland have increased the acreage to 138, with over 60 species of birds recorded.

At top of rise, in open area, turn right past barrier and left into rising gravel drive, to shortly pass 'Rourke's Drift' (beware of Zulus!) At top of incline by deep ditches, turn right to follow way-marked woodland path. At point where gap in trees on right gives glimpses of fine view, bear left along gravel path, soon descending steeply into gully. Way continues along enclosed path, with field on right sweeping up towards the fine wooded knoll of Beech Hill.

At green field gate on right, path widens into gravel track bearing left to reach road opposite Ambarrow Farm. Turn left along road, passing Ambarrow Lodge. Where road turns left, our circuit is complete, so continue ahead on footpath returning to start.

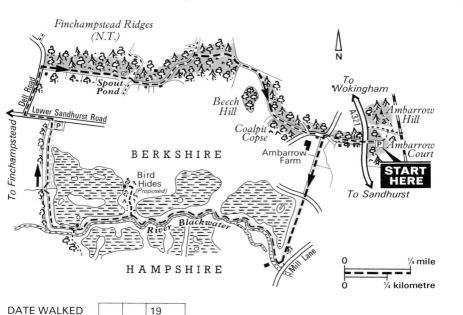

DATE WALKED | | 19 |

Although few signs remain today of the house, Ambarrow Court was a substantial Victorian mansion built on this site in 1885 by a Col. Harvey, whose widow lived here until her death in 1932, when the property was sold. In her will, Mrs Harvey left the adjoining Ambarrow Hill, some 14 acres of woodland, to the National Trust. So far, all efforts to discover the origin of this conical shaped hill have failed. It is not believed, as might be supposed, to be man-made. A footpath from the corner of the car-park leads directly to the summit.

Near Beech Hill.

Heath Warren and Eversley Church   Ramble 5

This walk follows paths and tracks through avariety of Forestry Commission woodland on Heath Warren. It then visits the historical focal point of old Eversley, the Church and former Rectory, closely associated with the Victorian writer and social commentator, Charles Kingsley, who was Rector here for over thirty years.

Distance: about 4 miles
OS Map: Pathfinder 1188
          'Mortimer and Arborfield'
Start: Small parking area at entry to
          Forestry Commission
          plantation,junction of
          unclassified road and south
          end of St Neots Rd - about 1
          mile west of Eversley Cross
          and 1 mile east of Bramshill.
          (Grid ref. 766614)

With back to road, pass through rails to right of metal gate. After a few yards on gravel track, fork right along grassy path which slowly rises, becoming sandy, to run along right-hand side of mature woodland. At prominent junction of five paths, turn right, down dip and up other side. Continue until end of woodland on left then, shortly beyond broad gravel track on left turn onto footpath through clear felled and replanted area, towards tall trees ahead.

The mature woodland in this part of Heath Warren, mainly Scots Pines, was planted in 1929. It is now fully grown and is being felled over a period up to 2001, in accordance with a careful conservation plan. The oppurtunity has been taken to re-open part of Eversley Footpath 7 which was obscured by Scots Pines. New planting will provide a wider selection of trees, including Douglas Fir, Sweet Chestnut, Cherry and possibly, some Sequioa.

Continue ahead through trees to join wide track along edge of forest - opposite small gravel lake. An ancient burial mound or tumulus lies immediately to the left at this point - Cudbury Clump. After 50 yards,(and similar distance before pylon ahead), bear left back into woodland to follow slowly rising bridleway - Welsh Drive - for nearly a mile, ignoring turnings on both sides.

The younger trees, along Welsh Drive, Scots Pine, Corsican Pine and some Birch, were planted about 20 years ago, after extraction of sand and gravel had reduced the ground level on the Heath by several feet.

Where track reaches highest point at 5-way crossing (notice one-time viewpoint

Welsh Drive.

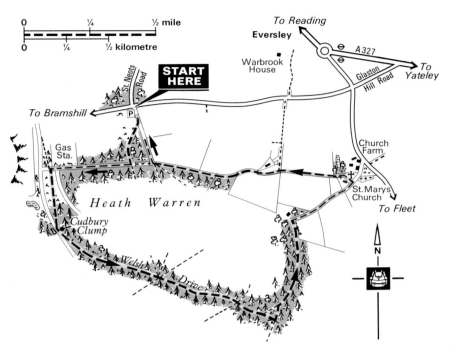

To Reading
Eversley
Warbrook
House
A 327
START HERE
To Bramshill
Glaston Hill Road
To Yateley
St. Neots Road
P
Gas Sta.
Church Farm
Heath Warren
St. Marys Church
Cudbury Clump
To Fleet
Welsh Drive
N

- periscope now required!), take first turning left along narrow path, with younger trees at first on left. Follow track into mature woodland, before merging with narrower descending path, soon with field on right. At bottom of woodland turn right between ornamental iron gate-posts and follow lane to pass house with ha-ha in front (the Old Rectory), before St Mary's Church. Notice here The Old Manor and Church Farm, where delightful old barns continue to serve a useful purpose.

Hopefully the Church will be open, as it is well worth a visit. Most of the present building was erected between 1724 and 1735, to designs by John James, one-time Surveyor to St Paul's Cathedral, who also built Warbrook House for himself, nearby in the village. Possible evidence of heathen worship on this site is the large sarsen stone which can be seen below the floor boards near the font. The most famous Rector here was Charles Kingsley - writer, teacher, academic, but essentially a caring parish priest, best remembered today, perhaps, as the author of 'The Water Babies'. There are memorials to him and his family in the Church, and he is buried close to the wall adjoining the Elizabethan house, which was the Rectory until 1971. Kingsley planted the Irish Yew trees which line the path to the porch. Shortly after his death in 1875, his daughter planted a seed she and her father had brought back from the United States, of the enormous Sequoia in the middle of the churchyard, His grave bears the inscription: 'Amavimus, Amamus, Amabimus' - 'We loved - We love - We shall love'.

To continue the walk, follow path around back of church, to leave churchyard through arch in yew hedge. Pass pond visible through trees on right and after stile follow the field-edge path ahead, through three fields with stiles. Then keep along inside edge of woodland with fine open views on right towards high ground on horizon. Driveway from left merges with path, along avenue of conifers. At meeting of forest tracks, bear right to return to start.

DATE WALKED [   ] [19]

Broad Oak and The Bury

This walk passes through the fields and meadows which closely encircle the ancient town of Odiham. Construction of the by-pass in 1979 has restored the air of peace and prosperity which has endured here since its origin as a Saxon Royal Manor. Today it has the rare status of an Outstanding Conservation Area.

Distance: about 3³/₄ miles
OS Map: Pathfinder 1204 'Basingstoke'
Start: Odiham Wharf Car Park at Colt Hill (Grid ref. 747517) approached from London Road, Odiham.

With your back to the by-pass, walk to the tow-path, close to red-brick Colt Hill Bridge which crosses the Basingstoke Canal here.

This was a busy wharf in the hey-day of the canal. The old cottage by the bridge was once a public house and still retains its original name - 'The Cricketers'. The Surrey & Hampshire Canal Society's boat - 'John Pinkerton' (named after the engineer who built the canal) sometimes operates from here. (See Stage 8 for further canal details.)

Turn left along tow-path, passing Galleon Marine on opposite bank (where holiday cruisers and day-boats can be hired in season). Pass under by-pass bridge and continue along canal bank to next bridge (Broad Oak). Pass under this bridge and after about 300 yards where end of small lake (Wilks Water) meets canal, take narrow path branching left. At end of lake, look left to see, beyond white garden gates, an elegant little house with decorative brick gables, known today as 'King John's Hunting Lodge'. It was built in 1730/40 as an ornament of nearby Dogmersfield Park and is now owned by the National Trust. (Not open to the public)

From a point about 25 yards in front of the white gates turn left into wood. Take left-hand of two minor paths which winds through trees of Odiham Common, returning shortly to Broad Oak Bridge. Now cross bridge and soon join tarmac road, with properties on right and green on left. At post-box outside Wincombe Cottage, turn left on gravel track. Pass between 'Greenwood' and 'Stream Cottage' into short enclosed path, to cross sleeper bridge and rails into meadow. Now turn right and follow field boundary. Leave meadow in corner, to cross series of stiles, past small pond on left and with stream close on right, finally to reach stile next to drive from bungalow on left and main road (A287).

Fishers Brook.

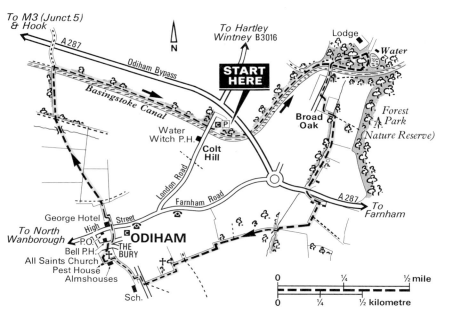

Carefully cross road, turn left down slope and after first property, turn right over stile to follow hedge on right. Cross plank bridge over ditch, continue to end of hedge on right and then bear half right to reach stile and wooden walk-way over stream in corner of meadow. Now follow field-edge path over one stile and through two left and right-hand turns, with wide views over fields to left, keeping hedge on right at all times. Eventually, follow track bearing right from corner of last field to join road.

Within a few yards, turn left across road into Buryfields and immediately turn right past houses at roadside. Pass Odiham Cottage Hospital on left, then down slope to fork left along tarmac drive, past Almshouses to reach little old brick cottage straight ahead - the Pest House. Follow path down through church-yard, past the brick and flint west front of All Saints Church.

The Almshouses and Pest House were built about 1625, the latter to house sufferers from the Plague and other infectious diseases - today it serves as a tiny museum in the care of the Odiham Society. The brick tower of All Saints was completed 1649 on a 14th century base. The four pinnacles were added in the 1800's. Hopefully, you will have time and opportunity to enjoy the splendours (the modern stained glass, for instance) and curiosities of this historic building. In fact the whole town is well worth a leisurely exploration.

Take the church path down into The Bury, the square in front of the church, and notice the old stocks and whipping post. Facing 'The Bell', turn right to pass between white posts and then turn left into narrow walled passage to right of Tudor 'Stoney Cottage'. Cross High St. and pass along right side of the 'George' (first licensed in 1510). Immediately in front of arched red-brick 'The Coach House', turn left through trellis arch, then right on gravel path. Follow narrow path between gardens to cross stile into open meadows stretching away in front. Bear slightly left to cross ditch to right of two trees on first field boundary, and then continue on same line through meadows ahead, once part of the mediaeval Royal Park. At top of third field, cross two stiles and follow left-hand fence. Leave field by stile to right of metal gate, cross canal bridge and immediately turn right to follow canal bank back to Colt Hill Bridge and car-park.

DATE WALKED [   ] [19   ]

Travel Information

BUS SERVICES

Bus Services in the **Windsor, Ascot, Bracknell and Crowthorne** area are currently operated mainly by the Berks Bucks Bus Company (The Bee Line). For detailed information contact the Bracknell Bus Station Travel Office. Tel: (0344) 424938
Open Mon - Fri   09.00 - 17.15
Sat   09.00 - 13.00

A map showing all the Bus and Rail services in **Hampshire** is obtainable from: The Passenger Transport Group, County Surveyor's Dept., Hampshire County Council, the Castle, Winchester, Hants. SO23 8UD

For information (during office hours only) telephone: (0962) 868944 or if phoning from within Hampshire dial 100 and ask for Freephone County Bus Line.

BRITISH RAIL AREA TELEPHONE ENQUIRIES

Aldershot and Guildford .... (0483) 755905
Basingstoke .... (0256) 464966
London, West *(24hr service)* .... (071) 262 6767
Reading .... (0734) 595911
Slough and Windsor .... (0753) 38621
Winchester .... (0703) 229393
Woking .... (0483) 755905

In case of delay (or an emergency) taxi services are available from Yateley, Eversley, Hartley Wintney and Odiham.